Ralph Linton

Leaders of Modern Anthropology Series
Charles Wagley, GENERAL EDITOR

RALPH LINTON

by Adelin Linton and Charles Wagley

Columbia University Press

1971 NEW YORK AND LONDON

Copyright © 1971 Columbia University Press
Library of Congress Catalog Card Number: 76-174708
ISBN: 0–231–03355–9 (*cloth*)
ISBN: 0–231–03398–2 (*paper*)
Printed in the United States of America

Preface

✤ This brief biography of Ralph Linton was written by his widow and by his former student and friend. Most of our information comes from firsthand knowledge of what Ralph Linton had to say and what he did. There are no "Linton papers" in the sense of an organized collection of his letters and diaries. Ralph Linton was not a prolific writer of letters, at least in the last two decades of his life. If he kept any diaries, they were probably in the form of field notes. Thus, this book is based upon the few documents we could muster, Linton's own writings and reports, and upon our own memories of the man. He may have seemed different to others who knew him well. There are certainly aspects and periods of his life about which we have little information. Yet, on the whole, the picture of Ralph Linton which emerges from the data we were able to collect seems consistent and relevant to the development of the man as a social scientist. We hope that this account and the selections from some of his writings that follow will help relate the man to his work and time, as well as contribute to the history of anthropology as a science. We also hope that our readers will go on to read Ralph Linton's own works, only a taste of which can be given here.

Adelin Linton
Charles Wagley

1970

Contents

Ralph Linton

PART I

Ralph Linton: The Man and his Work

Ralph Linton, who was born in 1893 and died in 1953, was one of the most distinguished anthropologists of his time. His career in anthropology covered a period during which this discipline underwent a dramatic transition; and Linton contributed fundamentally to its change. It might almost be said that it was Linton and several of his contemporaries, Robert Redfield, Melville Herskovits, Lloyd Warner, Ruth Benedict, and Margaret Mead, who brought anthropology in the United States out of the museums and into the mainstream of the social sciences.

During his lifetime, he received practically all of the honors that could be bestowed upon an anthropologist of his day. At various times he represented his profession on the National Research Council, on the Social Science Research Council, and on the American Council of Learned Societies. He was elected to the American Academy of Sciences; and in 1937 he was vice-president of the American Association for the Advancement of Sciences. From 1939 to 1944 he edited the *American Anthropologist*, and from 1938 to 1944 he was

1

chairman of the Anthropology Department at Columbia University. In 1946 he was appointed Sterling Professor of Anthropology at Yale University, and in that same year he was president of the American Anthropological Association. In 1951 he was awarded the Viking Fund Medal for his outstanding contribution to general anthropology. In 1953 he delivered the Thomas William Salmon Lectures to the American Medical Association on the subject of "Culture and Mental Disorders." He was only the second person to be chosen for this honor who was not an M.D. When he died he had been designated to receive in 1954 the Huxley Medal of the Royal Anthropological Institute of Great Britain and Ireland; he would have been the second American ever to receive this award.

When Linton began his career just before World War I, anthropology was taught in the United States at about a half dozen universities only. Most anthropological research was centered in museums such as the Smithsonian Institution, the American Museum of Natural History in New York, and the Field Museum in Chicago. Some of the large universities which offered courses in anthropology, such as Harvard, Yale, the University of California at Berkeley, and Pennsylvania, had museums of their own; Columbia University, where Franz Boas reigned, was closely connected to the American Museum of Natural History and for a time with the Museum of the American Indian in New York. At that time, anthropology was in a sense an isolated discipline. It was isolated from psychology, sociology, political science, and economics by its heritage from natural history. It was even isolated from history, despite its historical bent, by its subject matter, namely nonliterate peoples, and by its relative neglect of documentary sources. Universities hardly knew what to do with such a discipline. Should it be placed among the Humanities, with the Natural Sciences, or (as it was at Columbia University for a time) in the Faculty of Physical Sciences? After all, anthropology dealt with history, prehistory, biology, social life, and the origins of human institutions. It was a rather esoteric science and there were few anthropologists in the United States—all of whom knew each other and were familiar with each other's work.

This does not mean that anthropology in the 1920s was an arid field or a science without outstanding accomplishments. Ralph Linton belonged to what might be called the third generation of anthropologists in the United States. There was an early group headed by such people as Lewis Henry Morgan (1818–1881), Frederick W. Putnam (1839–1915), and Daniel G. Brinton (1837–1899). Franz Boas (1858–1942) came to the United States in 1889 and became the outstanding American anthropologist of his time. These men were followed by a second generation of anthropologists who were mainly students of Putnam and Boas: Alfred Kroeber, Robert Lowie, Edward Sapir, Clark Wissler, Alexander Goldenweiser, Paul Radin, Ronald Dixon, and others. At that time, American anthropology was marked by its holistic approach to the study of man—a concern with biology, linguistics, archeology, and social life. American anthropology still aspires to this holistic approach, but at that time it was possible for men like Boas, Kroeber, Lowie, Sapir, and others to have a firm grasp on the entire field and to make contributions in the several subdisciplines of anthropology.

When Linton began his career, American anthropology had already broken with nineteenth-century theories of unilineal evolution such as those of Lewis Henry Morgan, Herbert Spencer, and others. This nineteenth-century concept of cultured evolution held that societies passed through a series of stages such as those postulated by Morgan— Savagery, Barbarianism, and Civilization—each of which was characterized by a series of basic institutions, social customs, and material inventions. Today a new interpretation of cultural evolution is widely held, generally called multilineal evolution and indicating the various lines of change that have occurred. The criticism of cultural evolution by Boas and his students was aimed at the unilineal schemes of Morgan and others which lacked empirical ethnographic and historical evidence. Likewise, American anthropology had generally rejected the extreme diffusionist theories of G. Elliot Smith, Franz Graebner, and their respective disciples. Each of these theorists rejected the evolutionary approach to the history of human culture but, in turn, each attempted to offer a theory for the growth of culture throughout the globe and throughout human history. Both believed in the essential uninventiveness of man and ascribed practically all of cultural

3

growth to diffusion of institutions, material traits, and social custom. Smith (and later his follower W. J. Perry) ascribed all cultural growth, except the barest minimum, to ancient Egypt.[1] Less exaggerated, the German diffusionists led by Graebner[2] and including such as W. Koppers and W. Schmidt, saw the origin of culture in several locales, probably in Asia. Each small group developed its own distinctive culture complex, which then spread as strata or "culture circles" (kulturkreise) around the world. The empirical research by American anthropologists could not support these grand theories, neither that of cultural evolution nor that of world-wide diffusion. Actually, there were no grand theories in American anthropology at that time unless one so designated the concept of "Cultural Areas," which classified cultures regionally—that is, upon natural environments and historically verified diffusion of culture traits within a given region.

At that time, American anthropology was particularly strong in field ethnography, actual excavations in archeology, and the study of primitive languages. The discipline was preoccupied with the collection of data—particularly with the study of the American Indians before the tribes disappeared or became acculturated. Linton had before him the example of Franz Boas, who collected literally thousands of pages of data on the people of the northwest coast of America; the "salvage" ethnographies of the Indians of the Great Plains, based mainly upon intensive interviews with elderly Plains Indians by Clark Wissler, Robert H. Lowie, Leslie Spier, Alfred L. Kroeber, Paul Radin, and others; the work of Frank G. Speck among the northern Algonquins of Canada; the research of J. R. Swanton on the Indians of the southeastern United States; and the archeological excavations of A. V. Kidder, which seemed to put order into the historical development of the Pueblo cultures of the Southwest. This does not mean that theory and synthesis were entirely lacking at the time. Lowie published his important book *Primitive Society* in 1920 and Kroeber's magnificent synthesis *Anthropology* appeared for the first time in

[1] G. ELLIOT SMITH, *In the Beginning: the Origin of Civilization*, New York, Morrow, 1928.
[2] F. GRAEBNER, *Methode der Ethnologie*, Heidelberg, 1911.

4

1923. In England Bronislaw Malinowski had just begun to publish the results of his field research on the Trobriand Islands. Yet, in the 1920s American anthropology was far from being in the mainstream of scholarship. It was most certainly not a career which could promise security or many rewards to an ambitious young scholar. There was a jocose saying among anthropologists in the late '20s that "You don't have to be crazy to become an anthropologist, but it sure helps." Another comment, credited to Malinowski, was "Anthropology is the study of man, embracing woman." However one felt about the validity of these observations, it was true that one needed a high degree of determination and dedication, as well as a natural curiosity and a sense of the romantic, to select anthropology as a career in those early days.

In Linton's lifetime, the role of anthropology in universities and its relationship to the whole field of human scholarship changed. Anthropology joined with psychology and psychoanalysis to contribute to the study of human socialization and the relationship of personality and culture. It had entered into the study of complex cultures through the study of modern communities which were integral parts of great nations. Anthropology had combined with and contributed to sociological theory through the study of primitive societies. Through its study of unwritten languages it had evolved theories of linguistics and methods of teaching languages. Anthropology had contributed to the study of international relations through its analysis of cultures other than our own—often non-Western such as Japan, China, India, and often non-capitalistic such as the Soviet Union. By 1953, when Linton died, anthropology was already taught at hundreds of colleges and universities; and anthropologists were making their contribution to hundreds of interdisciplinary research projects in the social and biological sciences. And, since Linton's death, the field has continued to grow in numbers and in scope. One no longer need be either crazy or romantic to seek anthropology as a career.

Ralph Linton was born in Philadelphia on February 27, 1893. He was christened Rolfe after a remote ancestor, John Rolfe, who married Pocahontas, but since this odd name caused confusion when he entered school, he adopted the more familiar name of Ralph. His parents, Isaiah W. Linton and Mary Elizabeth Gillingham, were of Quaker ancestry. The Lintons came from Devonshire and received their land grants from William Penn. The Gillinghams arrived somewhat later. Isaiah Linton was a widower with twin sons when he married Elizabeth Gillingham, thirty years old at the time and considered an old maid in those days. She had been living with her semi-invalid mother, a woman happy in the belief that she had an unpaid companion for life and who never forgave Isaiah for carrying off her daughter.

Throughout his life Linton harbored considerable bitterness about his unhappy childhood and reminisced about it frequently to his friends. He attributed many of his personality traits and interests to the influence of his early experiences. Of course, one's memories of childhood are selective and frequently distorted. Although Linton was a convivial man who thoroughly enjoyed social contacts, he had a tendency to discount pleasurable experiences and to brood over situations in which he felt he had been slighted or treated unjustly. This characteristic undoubtedly colored his remembrances of his childhood, for he admitted that he had a comfortable home and was not deprived or unloved. Most young children accept the conditions of their life unquestioningly, and a more pliant and less egocentric boy could have been quite content in Ralph's circumstances. But he apparently battled from the start with his stern and authoritarian father. His mother was a gentle and loving woman but, as a good Victorian wife, allowed her husband to rule the household. Ralph's grandmother petted and spoiled him but the boy believed that she did this just to annoy his father. His half brothers were so much older than he that they gave him little companionship or support.

Linton's parents began their married life in Philadelphia. Their first child, a daughter, died shortly after Ralph was born. The family then moved into the home of Mrs. Linton's mother in Moorestown, New Jersey, where the three generations lived together until Mrs. Gillingham's death. Ralph attended the Friends School in Moorestown, where, he has said, he was not popular with his classmates. He was a fat, red-haired boy, disinterested and inept at sports and outstandingly bright in the classroom, except in spelling and arithmetic, two subjects he could never master. The other boys called him "Fats" and "Red" and since he could not tolerate what he considered to be ridicule, he did not attempt to participate in their pastimes but spent his spare time reading or wandering alone in the countryside, where he collected arrowheads, minerals, and biological specimens. To a boy with his romantic nature and lively mind, the Quaker drabness of his home proved very frustrating. Everything in the Linton house had to be both of good quality and plain. To gratify his yearning for color the boy decorated his own room with pots of fuchsias and the dried skins of snakes which he had caught. These colorful objects were God's handiwork and therefore acceptable.

The family set an ample table, and food as well as books provided compensations. Isaiah Linton owned a chain of restaurants in Philadelphia, and his day began early so that he could get to the Philadelphia markets when they opened to buy supplies. Breakfast was at five o'clock and he insisted that all the family be present, except for the grandmother, who spent her mornings in bed. Linton recalled with considerable bitterness the cold winter mornings when he had to crawl out of bed shivering at four-thirty, and later, stuffed with pancakes and sausages, read by lamplight until it was time to go to school.

The boy found another outlet for his craving for color and romance in the friendship he formed with J. W. Beath, an elderly jeweler in Philadelphia. Mr. Beath allowed the boy to pore over his collections of jewelry and unset stones and gave him instruction in gemology. As a result Linton developed an interest in gems which continued throughout his life. As soon as he could afford to do so, he began a collection of opals and varicolored sapphires. In the 1940s when he visited Rio de Janeiro he was fascinated by the great variety of Brazilian semiprecious stones and delighted the jewelers both with his knowledge and his purchases.

Young Ralph had little time to devote to his hobbies, however, for his father believed that young boys should be kept busy at useful tasks. As soon as he was big enough to push a lawnmover, Ralph was required to do the yard work on the spacious grounds of his home. From the age of twelve, he was expected to serve as a bus boy in his father's restaurants during weekends and summer vacations. He detested and resented this work, particularly as he knew that he was required to work not as a financial necessity for the family but as a disciplinary measure on his father's part. His only pleasant memory of the restaurant experience was that he made friends with the meat cutter, who instructed him in his craft, assuring him that a college education might be very well but that if one really knew how to handle meat one could always get a job. Linton was proud of this skill. When he was a guest at a dinner party where the host was mangling a good roast, he would watch with such a fixed and pained expression that the host would ask him if he would like to carve. Linton usually accepted with alacrity. Undoubtedly his proficiency with the knife served him in good stead also when he took up wood carving in the Marquesas Islands.

Ralph always received payment for his work, but the money was put into a savings account which he was not allowed to touch. His father was doubtless trying to teach the boy industry and thrift but the son proved to be counter-suggestible to this as to most of his father's decrees. He was always a hard worker but only at things which he wanted to do. Although a Quaker horror of debt was instilled in him by his family, he always spent money as fast as he could make it and considered savings or investments as wasted opportunity. After his death when the safe-deposit box which he owned jointly with his wife was formally opened in the presence of an officer of the bank, a representative from the probate court, and the estate lawyer, they were somewhat startled to discover that the only assets belonging to Linton in the box were six packages of opals and sapphires and fifty shares of the Quansoo Shellfish Farm, John Whiting's venture into oyster raising at Martha's Vineyard which never paid a dividend and was finally washed away in a hurricane.

In 1911 Linton entered Swarthmore College, another Quaker school. He wanted to major in biology but his father thought there were few job opportunities in this field and insisted that he take up engineering instead. "My older sons will inherit the business," he said, "and you will have to make your own way." Linton had no desire to become a restauranteur but neither had he any bent for engineering. College opened up new vistas for the young man, not particularly along academic lines. On campus, for the first time, he formed close friendships with his fellow students and also discovered that he could be attractive to girls. He was a handsome young man at this time. Away from his mother's table and no longer needing food as a solace for frustration he slimmed down. His red hair had mellowed to a mild chestnut and he was a well-built six-footer. Linton has said that the weekend that he spent at the home of one of his classmates was the first time that he realized that family atmosphere could be delightful and harmonious and that parents and children could have warm, happy relationships with one another. He found most of his social contacts at college a new and pleasant experience but his classes bored him and he gave little time to his studies. At the end of the year he was failing in half of his subjects and was expelled from the college. However, Spencer Trotter, his science professor, and Charles Goddard in the English Department recognized his talents (he had done well in the two courses which interested him) and persuaded the authorities to take him back on probation. This was not sufficient for Isaiah Linton, however, who affirmed that he could not afford to send a son to college to fritter away his time, and he demanded that the young man quit college and go to work. Linton got himself a job on a truck farm that summer (he never again worked in the restaurants), saved enough money for his tuition, and worked his way through his Sophomore year as a biology major. That spring he had top grades in every subject. His father relented and financed the rest of his college education.

The following summer Linton joined an archeological expedition to New Mexico and Colorado. This was his first contact with anthropology, for no courses in this subject were offered at Swarthmore. He joined the group because it was an opportunity to get away from home and see something of the rest of the country, not because he had any special interest in southwestern archeology. He was just a pick-and-shovel man working for his keep.

The group worked in the Mesa Verde and then went on into southern Colorado where, in Johnson Canyon, they came upon a cliff house which had not been entered since its inhabitants had fled some

9

1,500 years earlier. The party rigged up a makeshift ladder to scale the entrance to the cave and Linton, as the youngest and most agile member of the group, was delegated to climb up and enter the house. As he neared the top the ladder began to crack. He managed to pull himself safely into the entrance of the house but the leader felt that it would be unsafe for him to attempt to descend. Linton's companions hoisted food and water and a blanket up to him and, promising to return the next morning with a stouter ladder, they departed, leaving Linton to spend the night alone in the house.

In the remaining daylight, he explored the premises. All was covered with a fine layer of powdery dust which had filtered down through the ages. In a pot on the hearth he found the remnants of a corn and rabbit stew; a blanket was half woven on its loom and a pair of worn sandals hung from a peg on the wall. However, there were no traces of human remains. The inhabitants had apparently fled hastily and never returned, why no one knows. Linton stripped wood from the old beams and built himself a fire. He was not a trained anthropologist and did not realize he might have been destroying important evidence. He sat at the entrance of the cave beside his fire while the sky turned to flaming orange behind the black mesas. This was a profound and mystical experience for the sensitive young man, and it was during this night spent with the ghosts of the past that he made up his mind that he was going to become an archeologist. The house was later investigated by proper anthropological methods in which Linton, as a very junior member of the expedition, had no special part. He did not try to make scientific notes but when he returned to Swarthmore he wrote a long poem about his night in the cliff house which won the first award in a regional collegiate contest.

The winter of his junior year, Linton obtained leave from college to accompany an expedition which was going to Guatemala to make moulds of the Maya monuments in Quiragua, an early Mayan site in the lowlands near the Caribbean coast where the great stelae stood deep in the humid jungle. This was Linton's first contact with people of another culture and he was much interested in the native workmen, most of whom were descendants of the Maya. In particular he was impressed with their fortitude and courage. He told the story of one workman who was bitten on the hand by a poisonous tree snake while he was cutting a path through the jungle growth. Without a moment's hesitation the man swung his machete and cut off his own hand. "If I hadn't done it, I'd be dead by now," the man explained. "There was no other way." This episode made a profound impression on Linton.

The heat in the jungle was so intense that the men found that they could work only at night by the light of flares, for the glue which they used for the moulds would not set in the heat of the day. When the moulds were completed, they were lashed to canoes and paddled out to a waiting ship and sent back to the United States, where the final casts were made. Linton did not see the finished product until many years later when, on a sabbatical leave from Yale, he visited the San Diego Museum where the casts of the eight-foot Quiragua figures stand in a semicircle in the rotunda. He said that it was like coming unexpectedly upon old friends.

In June of 1915, Linton graduated from Swarthmore College, and was awarded the Phi Beta Kappa, quite an achievement for a student who had flunked out his Freshman year. Soon after graduation he married his classmate and college sweetheart, Josephine Foster. During the summer of that year he took part in the excavations near Haddonfield, New Jersey, for the Museum of the University of Pennsylvania. This work resulted in his first professional publication in collaboration with B. W. Hawkes, "A Pre-Lenape Site in New Jersey" (1917), in which is described the first Archaic site to be discovered south of New England.[3]

In 1915–1916, Linton was a graduate student in anthropology at the University of Pennsylvania, from which he received his M.A. in 1916. His main interest was still in archeology but he took courses that year in ethnology under Frank Speck, his first work in this field. The summer of 1916 he returned to field archeology, excavating at Aztec, New Mexico, under the auspices of the American Museum of Natural History.

For the academic year 1916–1917, Linton transferred to Columbia

[3] ANTHROPOLOGICAL PUBLICATIONS of the Museum of the University of Pennsylvania 4, No. 3.

University. This school offered very little in archeology but Linton was eager to work with the famous Franz Boas. He had only one formal course with Boas that year, a course in anthropological linguistics. This was one subdiscipline in anthropology in which Linton never manifested much interest and for which he apparently had little aptitude. He failed to distinguish himself in this class and never became one of the devoted students who clustered around Boas. The master considered him a poor student; and Linton, in fact, never formed strong attachments or became a disciple of any of his teachers. Perhaps his resentment of his father was responsible for his life-long reactions against authoritarianism.

In April 1917, while Linton was studying at Columbia, war was declared. He recalled that his first instincts were to join up at once, but he had been reared in the Quaker tradition of pacifism, he had a wife, and a year of schooling to complete, so he held off. This conflict of emotion may have contributed to his undistinguished academic record at Columbia. That summer Linton and his wife went off to southern Illinois, where he was engaged to assist in the excavation of Indian mounds. When he completed this task in August, he could resist no longer. He sent his wife back East to her family and entrained to Chicago to enlist. He was assigned to the 42nd Division, which came to be known as the Rainbow Division because it was made up of men from many different states. It was the first division to reach France and participated in five of the six major battles of the war. Felons awaiting trial in the Chicago jails were told that if they enlisted their cases would be dropped. They did so almost to a man and Linton has said that these men became some of the finest soldiers in the division. The Rainbow Division was known for its *esprit de corps* and Linton was anxious to embark for France with this unit, to which he had become devoted during training. When he was recommended for Officers' School he falsified his questionnaire, saying that he was a graduate of Friends High School in Moorestown, New Jersey, and that his occupation was that of farmer, and so was passed over and embarked for France with his division.

Linton's eagerness to enlist does not seem to have been due entirely to patriotism and certainly not to conscience. His action was highly dismaying to his parents and he was read out of the Moorestown Friends Meeting.[4] The Friends could accept one of their members submitting if he was drafted, although Quakers could be excused from service on religious grounds; but voluntary enlistment without even consulting one's parents was too much for the elders to accept. It would seem that Linton envisioned the war as a great adventure, as many young men did in those more innocent times. He also regarded it as an anthropological laboratory, a field trip where one could observe many sorts of men under unusual conditions. He was fascinated to find himself in close association with men of various classes and backgrounds and to see them welded into a cadre of loyalties and mutual concern. Although Linton fought a tough war (he was both wounded and gassed at various times), he considered the war a rewarding experience and afterwards lost neither his romantic nor his anthropological point of view toward it. (Witness his monograph *Totemism in the A.E.F.,* which is included in this volume.)

He wrote poetry all during the war, frequently brief poignant verses scribbled on the backs of envelopes in shell holes. Some of his war poetry was published in the overseas *Stars and Stripes.* Some, which he included in letters to his family, were sent by his mother to various American magazines, which almost invariably published them. Although he achieved a reputation of sorts as a young war poet, Linton never took his verses seriously nor kept a file of them, and after the war he abandoned the writing of poetry. Linton ended the war as a liaison corporal, a highly hazardous job in which a man traveled alone through enemy territory carrying messages.

Although the war ended in November 1918, Linton did not return until the autumn of 1919. He had spent considerable time in a hospital after the end of hostilities and then in occupation forces in France. As he planned to continue his graduate work for the Ph.D. at Columbia and was already late for registration, he hurried into New York from Fort Dix as soon as possible and, still in uniform, called upon Boas. It is well known that Boas was against United States participation in World War I (he was a German by birth and

[4] LINTON WAS later reinstated and retained his membership in the Moorestown Friends meeting until after the death of his mother.

training). Boas received Linton coldly. He had never held him in
high regard as a student and was doubtless irritated by the American
uniform. Linton has reported that Boas informed him that he might
register at Columbia but that it was doubtful that he could earn a
doctoral degree there. Linton left Boas's office and took the first train
to Boston, where he enrolled as a candidate for the Ph.D. at Harvard.
It is ironic that the next time Linton entered Boas's office he was
arriving as Boas's probable replacement as Chairman of the Anthropology Department at Columbia.

Linton claimed to be the only student who ever received a Ph.D.
from Harvard with less than one year in residence, as he entered late
and left early to do research on Mesa Verde ruins in southwestern
Colorado. He used to say that Harvard had to change the rules after
he left. Linton did not form any close associations with either fellow
students or professors during this year. Coming directly from the
battlefront to this Ivy League university apparently gave the returned
soldier a feeling of social inferiority. He maintained that Harvard
considered him uncouth and rude, and perhaps it did. He had never,
at this point, given much attention to social amenities and in addition
he was no doubt in a disturbed state. The rebuff he had received from
Boas must have rankled, his wife had left him, and his father had died
while he was overseas, so he was not in a happy frame of mind when
he entered Harvard.

Linton's closest friend at Harvard seems to have been Ernest
Hooton, who later became the most famous physical anthropologist
in the United States, but was then a young instructor. Linton also
had a great admiration for Alfred Tozzer, the well-known scholar in
the field of Mayan studies. Some of Linton's later work shows the
influence of the thinking of Roland Dixon, whose critical appraisal
of the mechanical diffusion theories of culture of the school of Clark
Wissler and others appeared in *The Building of Cultures* some years
later (1923). Apparently Linton was appreciated intellectually, if not
socially, at Harvard, for he was awarded his Ph.D. degree in 1925, and
through his Harvard connections was able to secure his first professional appointments in anthropology.

14

After his abbreviated year at Harvard, he was back in the field at once. First, he returned to Mesa Verde National Park, where he assisted in excavating and reconstructing Square Tower House. During this period he discovered and excavated Earth Lodge A, the first Basket Maker III structure to be identified in the region. In the fall of 1920, he was sent by the B. P. Bishop Museum of Honolulu to join an expedition to the Marquesas Islands in the eastern Pacific. The expedition was led by Dr. E. S. C. Handy, who was to undertake the ethnographic study of Marquesan society. Linton was engaged as an archeologist. But in fact,

❖ *Linton found the living Marquesans more interesting than the archeological remains of their ancestors. The trip was a turning point in his career, and from that time forward his attention was directed primarily to living people and their cultures. Although he never "turned his back" on archeology or "material culture," they were increasingly overshadowed by his consuming interest in social structure, social process, and personality."* [5] ❖

Linton wrote two reports resulting from the expedition. *The Material Culture of the Marquesas Islands* (1923) was his doctoral dissertation, and in 1925 he published *Archaeology of the Marquesas Islands* (1925). Dr. Handy published *The Native Culture of the Marquesas* (1923) and *Marquesan Legends* (1930), which Linton drew upon in his own later interpretations of Marquesan society and culture.[6]

Linton's memories of his Marquesas sojourn were particularly vivid. After a brief stay in Tahiti, Dr. and Mrs. Handy and Linton sailed to the Marquesas, where they established themselves in the town of Atuona on Hiva Oa island, the capital of the group of eleven islands. Dr. and Mrs. Handy found quarters in the home of Ben Varney, who

---

[5] JOHN GILLIN, "Ralph Linton," in *American Anthropologist*, Vol. 56 (1954), 276.

[6] RALPH LINTON, "Marquesan Culture," in Abram Kardiner, *The Individual and His Society*, New York, Columbia University Press, 1939, pp. 137–96.

ran the general store and represented the shipping line for the islands. Linton was domiciled with Rev. Paul Vernier, a French missionary. Both he and the Handys took their meals with the Varneys. Linton wrote to his mother that Mrs. Varney, who was half Polynesian, was a splendid woman and an excellent cook. By the time Handy and Linton arrived, Marquesan culture was badly broken and the islands were sparsely populated. The southern cluster of the Marquesas Islands had been discovered in the late sixteenth century by a Spanish navigator and the northern group in 1795 by an American navigator, Captain Ingraham, who named the group the Washington Islands. For a time, it seemed that the islands would be annexed to the United States, but by 1842 they were ceded to France. Despite such long contact with Western man, the Marquesans resisted white influence and were among the last of the Polynesian groups to be Christianized. Western diseases and a deliberate attempt at self-genocide had decimated the people. When the Marquesans were finally forced to submit, they adopted the only means of dignified and effective resistance which was open to them—they ceased to breed. This was a perfectly deliberate measure, the people preferring extinction to subjugation. "I visited," Linton wrote, "many villages populated entirely by persons of early middle age to old age with not a single child in the group." [7] Yet, because of their resistance to Western culture, some of the native life remained, and there were older men and women who remembered the former days.

The Marquesas Islands had been enshrined in literature and in art. They were the setting of Herman Melville's adventure *Typee*, which tells of the author's capture by a Marquesan cannibal tribe (Linton confirmed the existence of cannibalism from old men who had practiced it). Melville tells how he was well treated and nursed back to health, however, by the Typee, and of his romantic experiences with native women. Then, at the turn of the century, Gauguin, who had been living and painting on Tahiti, came to the Marquesas Islands, where he died at Atuona in 1903. Linton, always an aesthete, was overwhelmed by the beauty and romance of the islands. The following is quoted from an essay he wrote in Hiva Oa.

[7] *Ibid.*, p. 137.

16

✥ We zigzagged back and forth through the coconut trees, our horses scrambling like cats, and at last rejoined the old road built by the French. This wound up the hillside, passing over and under great outcrops of black rock. We passed through a zone of stunted guavas and wind-twisted mango trees and came out on a treeless hill covered with golden brown fern and the pale yellow clumps of a species of bamboo. A stiff climb brought us to the crest and here we paused to look back. The sea lay far below, smooth and glistening like silk and we could see headland after headland, fantastic shapes of black rock with tiny bands of white at their feet. The coconut trees of Taoa resembled a bed of moss and beyond them, encircling the valley rose the sheer wall of Temtiu, his head veiled in clouds.

We crossed the crest and found ourselves in a forest of ironwood trees with a carpet of soft brown needles underfoot and the wind singing the same old song he sings in the pines at home. The leaves overhead made a delicate tracery against the sky and here and there a break in the trees gave us a glimpse of the forest below, a softly curving sweep of grayish green as fine in texture as the fur of an animal.

We left the ironwoods, winding on through valley after valley and came out again into great slopes of scrub and fern. Sometimes, far below we could see the darker growth of banyans and mangoes at the foot of the valleys where they meet the sea. Several times we passed through the ruins of old villages, their stone paepaes (platforms) overgrown and ruinous, and once the trail passed the pavement of an old feast place, fallen into decay and its very name forgotten. At last we saw three native houses. Fiu [his companion] explained that a man stayed here sometimes to look after the pigs which roamed the hills, but no one lived here regularly. The tribes which had once inhabited these valleys in their thousands are gone utterly, without leaving a single descendant. ✥

Handy's chief interest was in religion, ceremonial, and mythology. He spent most of his time in Atuona on Hiva Oa. There he could have native informants brought to him; and could record myths and folktales in native text, and query their memories for the old concepts of religion and ceremonial. Linton was more mobile, ranging about the islands trying to make friends with people and looking for archeological remains. He formed a particularly strong friendship with one young Marquesan, Fiu, who adopted him as his blood brother with all of the proper ritual. Linton thus became a son in Fiu's household and Fiu accompanied him on his explorations of the islands, acting as guide and interpreter. In his travels about Hiva Oa and other islands, he met and became friendly with many natives and was able to observe their current culture patterns as well as hear of the old times from the elders. These informal ethnographic observations were duly inscribed in his notebooks but he did not organize or publish any of this material until he described Marquesan society and culture in his collaborative work with Abram Kardiner.[8]

The archeology of the Marquesas Islands proved rather unrewarding, especially for a single archeologist. The Marquesans did not have pottery, which is most often the key to stratigraphic and temporal sequences in archeology. They used stone for the most part only for *paepae*, or house platforms, which although enduring are not particularly revealing except to show the old settlement pattern. Although mountainous, the Marquesas are also tropical; and the old village sites were heavily overgrown with vegetation. It would have taken an army of excavators to uncover Marquesan village sites. Yet, Linton did produce a highly respectable archeological survey, which was published in 1925 by the Bishop Museum. On the other hand, the material culture was rich, especially Marquesan work in wood. They made not only canoes, but also carved wooden bowls, weapons, and other objects. There was a special group of master craftsmen, the *tuhungas*, who were highly respected carvers gifted also with magical and ritual powers. They also made tapa cloth, wove mats, and carved coconut shells for use as utensils. Linton became extremely interested in these Polynesian crafts. He undertook a study of material culture, past and present, and collected widely for the Bishop Museum.

Linton and Fiu traveled extensively around the villages and meager settlements of Hiva Oa. Linton collected objects and talked to the

[8] *Ibid.*, pp. 139–96.

people, mostly the old people, for he was absorbed in trying to reconstruct the old culture. Another section of his previously quoted journal is typical of Linton's Marquesas explorations:

✥ *It was almost dark when we reached the bottom of the valley of Hanamenu but the entire permanent population, consisting of two men and one old and one young woman, turned out to welcome us. The old woman was the last member of the once powerful Hanamenu tribe. She regarded me with considerable suspicion at first, fearing that I would disturb the remains of her ancestors. The first night when we gathered in the after-supper circle, she sat far off on her own paepae. The second night she came up on the porch and squatted beside me. On the last afternoon of my stay, I discovered three tapa beaters of an unusual form while poking around in the rubbish of a deserted house and it developed that these had belonged to her. I offered her the magnificent sum of ten francs for the three and she at once concluded that I had taken pity on her age and poverty. She not only sold them to me but returned shortly after with a tiny poi pounder, used to prepare the food of young children, a shell for scraping bread-fruit, and an ornament of hair and human bone, all of which she gave me. From that moment on, her tongue never ceased to wag. She told me about the good old times when whaling ships stopped for water and she and the other girls would swim out and live aboard for the whole time of the ship's stay. Her father had been a priest and she recited the tale of creation with its ages of slowly changing darkness which gave birth at last to the sea, which gave birth to land. She had many other tales of the lore of her people.* ✥

In *Typee*, Herman Melville describes the boarding of an arriving sailing vessel by Marquesan "mermaids" and their free and licentious behavior aboard, but in the mid-nineteenth century when Melville visited the Marquesas such valleys as Hanamenu held tribes (Typee was one) of well over a thousand people; each tribe had a huge feasting place and dance ground (the *tohua*) built near the chief's household, and made level by moving many tons of rock. Scattered about were the individual households, each with its level platform. The household was not just a house but rather an elaborate compound. There was the dwelling house at the rear, in which were comfortable beds of ferns and grass and woven mats. There was in addition a storehouse for food which also held sacred taboo objects and a separate house for cooking and eating. The Marquesans were polyandrous; thus, each household consisted of a main husband, the wife or wives and a series of subsidiary husbands who shared the sexual favors of the wife or wives with the main husband. Melville describes such marital arrangements, and when Linton visited the Marquesas some polyandrous households persisted. With the help of old informants, Handy's ethnographic research, and his own observations, Linton was able to write a graphic account of the Marquesan household many years later.

On another of his trips into the interior of Hiva Oa, Linton discovered a shallow cave which housed an image of a rain god. The god seemed to be abandoned. There were no signs of any offerings or human visitation. It was probably the image of a tribal god which in the past had been in charge of a special priest and to which sacrifice (even human sacrifice) was made. Linton decided to add this abandoned image to the collection he was making for the Bishop Museum. However, none of the people in the village would help him carry the idol down the mountain and it was too big for him to manage alone. He was finally able to hire men from another valley to bring the statue down to Atuona. The day he set it up in his house black thunderclouds rolled up and it began to rain. The rain continued in torrents all day, and the river began to rise and lap at the banks where the houses stood. Linton's adopted brother came to him and said, "The people are saying that you caused this rain by bringing the god into the village. If the river keeps rising and floods the village they are going to be very angry with you. You had better do something." Linton told how he then set the god up in the village street and addressed him in loud tones, saying that he had been abandoned for years up in the mountains, eroded by weather, eaten by insects, and forgotten by his people. Now the white man proposed to take him in a big ship to a fine building in a great town where he would be set up in a glass case and many people would come to worship and admire him. The rain stopped and the river flood subsided. When it came time to ferry the statue out to the ship, there was no trouble in finding native men to help move it.

There is a sequel to this story. Some years later the Bishop Museum traded this Marquesan image of a rain god to the Field Museum of Chicago, where Linton had become a curator of ethnology. It was in August when the object arrived in Chicago and there had been a drought in Illinois which was endangering the corn crop. The very day that the rain god was installed in the Field Museum a gentle all-day rain started. Linton happened to be dining that night at the Quadrangle Club at the University of Chicago. He regaled his dinner companions with the story. A newspaper reporter at a nearby table eavesdropped on the conversation. The next day the story appeared in one of the Chicago newspapers. Crowds of people came to the museum to see this image that could make rain in both the Marquesas Islands and in Illinois and several "rainmakers" around the country wrote to the museum asking if they could borrow the image of the Marquesan deity for the relief of drought-harrassed regions.

In the Marquesas Linton not only collected objects of material culture, but he also learned Marquesan craftwork. All Marquesan men knew how to make the tools and utensils they needed in daily life, but those who were truly expert in creating beautiful things were highly respected. These master craftsmen, called *tuhungas*, made up a special occupational-priestly class. They not only knew the artistic and mechanical techniques for carving in wood and occasionally in stone, but also the proper chants and magical practices considered necessary for the creation of any object. "A food bowl made without the proper magical ritual would be just a food bowl. It would have no real place in the universe and consequently no value." [9] Such well-made objects were personified and they were given names in the same way as people. When Linton learned that the *tuhungas* took paying pupils to train in the skills and the rituals of wood carving, he enrolled as a pupil of Hapuani, one of the last of the old wood carvers. This was a very effective method of involving himself in the culture and

[9] *Ibid.*, p. 146.

Linton was also deeply interested in Marquesan artistic conventions. He frequently said that one of the proudest days of his life was when he executed a carved wooden bowl for a native and was paid for it with a live pig. His "graduation exercise" was a fetish figure executed in low relief. Linton kept this carving on his wall throughout his life, always with little elephants between its feet "to make it feel important." He gave it the name of Tapu Tapu Atea and claimed that it was his personal fetish. He attributed a number of odd occurrences to the magical powers of Tapu Tapu Atea. All of his students and friends came to know this carving and often brought elephants to propitiate it.

Linton knew that Paul Gauguin had died in Atuona some seventeen years before. Being a great admirer of this painter, who was just beginning to be widely known in the United States, he set out to learn what he could about Gauguin's Marquesan life. He found that Ben Varney had known the painter quite well. It was Varney who had made arrangements for the house which Gauguin had built in the valley. Gauguin bought his supplies at Varney's store, as he existed largely on imported canned goods and French wine, abjuring native foods. Pastor Vernier, in whose house Linton had lived, had been Gauguin's only close friend in the French colony. The missionary had disapproved strongly of Gauguin's way of life but respected his intellect. The two had many long talks together. Gauguin wished to give his friend a painting and invited him to come to his house and choose any one he wanted, but Vernier always managed to evade the invitation. He regarded Gauguin's paintings as sensual daubs and felt that to hang one on his wall would endanger his position in the community. Vernier must have regretted this decision, for he lived to see Gauguin's paintings valued at thousands of dollars. Hopuani, Linton's teacher in wood carving, knew of Gauguin as a fellow *tuhunga* but they had never met. Gauguin, although he had a succession of native mistresses and servants and always took the natives' side against the French in any dispute, manifested, strangely enough, scant interest in the native artists or their work.

Linton tried to discover where Gauguin was buried but no one seemed to know. He was told that the natives had carried off the body

22

and buried it and that the gendarmes had come to burn Gauguin's house on the grounds that it was contaminated. Gauguin had in fact suffered from a variety of diseases. People told Linton that the walls of his house had been painted with murals, mostly pornographic; and the lintels and the doorpost had been carved by the artist himself. The local officials also came to regret this act when they learned that they could have made a fortune from the sale of this art work. In any case, Linton finally found two of the men who had helped bury Gauguin. Each took him independently to an overgrown section of the French cemetery where one could just faintly tell by pushing aside the vegetation that there was a grave. However, no marker had ever been erected. Linton told how he found a huge lump of coral and had it moved to the cemetery and placed at what he thought to be the head of Gauguin's grave. He carved "Paul Gauguin 1848–1903" on this crude marker. Bent Danielsen's book *Gauguin in the South Seas* [10] contains a color photograph of Gauguin's grave showing the stone marker which the French government put there some time after Linton's stay in the Marquesas. Danielsen's caption reads: "After being long overgrown with weeds and then for many years disfigured with an ugly slab of cement [sic], Gauguin's grave has recently been marked by this slightly better stone cover." [11] If Ralph Linton had not set up that "ugly slab of cement," the grave would undoubtedly have been so overgrown that it could never have been located.

Ralph Linton's visit to the Marquesas Islands was both a highly successful anthropological research venture and a moving personal experience. He wrote two basic field reports for the Bishop Museum which brought him recognition in the scientific world. His close relationship with the Marquesan people, no matter how broken their culture, turned his interest from archeology to living nonliterate cultures and provided him with a body of knowledge that he later used in many of his theoretical formulations. When employing Marquesan culture as an example in his lectures or in his writing, he could always

[10] BENT DANIELSEN, *Gauguin in the South Seas*, New York, Doubleday and Co., 1966.
[11] *Ibid.*, p. 313.

bring that primitive society and culture back to life. In the Marquesas
he had his first experience of living on intimate terms with a non-
Western culture, which provided him with a truly important understanding of the sort which is basic for all anthropologists.

On his return from the Marquesas in 1922, Linton accepted a post
as assistant curator at the Field Museum of Chicago, now the Chicago
Museum of Natural History. Before going to Illinois, he went to New
York, where he tried to look up old friends, and made contact with
Margaret McIntosh, a Swarthmore classmate and close friend of his
former wife. After a brief courtship they were married and the new
wife accompanied her husband to Chicago. Linton's only child, David
Hector Linton, was born there a few years later.

Linton's first marriage had been the culmination of a college romance. The couple lived together for only two years while Linton was
a struggling graduate student on two different campuses. When Linton went voluntarily off to the war, the young wife was unable to cope
with loneliness, formed a new liaison, and asked Linton for a divorce
while he was fighting in France. His second marriage was never a harmonious one, at least according to Linton, and it deteriorated further
after the couple went to Wisconsin. In 1932 they agreed to a trial
separation, Margaret Linton and David going to New York while
Linton remained at his teaching post in Madison. The couple were
never reunited and obtained a divorce in 1934. In 1935 Linton married
Adelin Hohlfeld, a young widow who was at the time a columnist and
book reviewer for the Madison *Capital Times*. This union proved to
be a close and enduring one.

Adelin Linton continued her newspaper work so long as the Lintons remained in Wisconsin. In New York, when Linton took on the
editorship of *American Anthropologist*, Adelin Linton took over the
technical editing of the journal. When the Lintons went to Yale,
Linton was the editor of the Viking Fund Publications and again
Adelin Linton did the routine editorial work for this series of monographs. It will be noted in the Bibliography that a number of items
are of joint authorship. This was not collaboration in the usual sense.
Linton would frequently be approached by magazine editors or book
publishers with requests for work of a popular nature. He had no
interest in this but would ask his wife if she would like to undertake

it, which she usually did. Sometimes such pieces were ghost written under Linton's name and sometimes both names appeared, but except for occasional information and advice, Linton did not concern himself with these publications, and all royalties and payments for such work went to Mrs. Linton. This casual use of his name is highly atypical for important scientists but another proof of Linton's unconventionality and lack of self-importance as an academician. In his serious scientific work, Linton was meticulous and Mrs. Linton never participated in it, except for *The Tree of Culture* (1955), which was only about two-thirds completed at the time of Linton's death. The lecture course on which *The Tree of Culture* was based had been transcribed through a grant from the Viking Fund. Because of his precarious health, Linton had made sure that the book would be completed by his wife in the event that he was unable to do so himself, and her name had always been on the contract for its publication. So, from the available notes and transcripts, Mrs. Linton completed the work.

At the Field Museum, Linton was officially curator of American Indian materials but he ranged over the whole of the museum's collections. This museum experience, combined with his field research in the Marquesan material culture, undoubtedly initiated the interest and sensitivity to artifacts and art objects which persisted throughout his life. In Chicago he also continued his interest in archeology, and in the summer of 1924 he took part in the excavation of the original Hopewell site of the so-called Mound Builder Culture in Ohio. Furthermore, he did not neglect American Indian ethnography. The Field Museum held rich archival material on the Pawnee, an Indian tribe of the Great Plains. This material had been collected by George A. Dorsey with the help of an educated half-blooded Pawnee named James R. Murie, who had worked earlier with Clark Wissler of the American Museum of Natural History and with Alice C. Fletcher, who also wrote on the Pawnee. Linton set to work organizing some of the unpublished data collected by Murie and Dorsey (he freely acknowledges his sources) in a series of bulletins and articles on the Pawnee which taken together form an important contribution to American Indian ethnography.[12]

In 1925 Linton was dispatched by the museum as a one-man Mar-

---

[12] Cf. LINTON bibliography in this volume.

shall Field Anthropological Expedition to Madagascar. His assignment was to make collections of material objects for the Field Museum and carry out an ethnographic survey of the various tribes of the island. The selection of Linton for this task and Madagascar as the site was not fortuitous, for Madagascar was inhabited by Malagasy-speaking peoples whose languages were closely related to the Malayo-Polynesian languages of Oceania. It was thought that Malayan peoples had probably supplanted the earlier Negroid people, and after establishing themselves in Madagascar they had received and partially assimilated a wave of people from the east coast of Africa. Having worked with one of the most eastern groups of people speaking Malayo-Polynesian languages, namely the Marquesans, Linton would now be able to work with the most western extension of people speaking a language of this stock.

Accompanied by his wife, Linton left Chicago in October of 1925 for France. His son, David, then two years old, was left with friends in the United States. Madagascar was, of course, a colony of France at the time, and the necessary permissions for museum collecting and ethnographic research had to be acquired. In December, the Lintons were able to sail from Marseilles, arriving in Tamatave, Madagascar, on January 17th, 1926. After two days in the port, they proceeded by train up the mountains to Tananarive, the capital city of the island, which is three thousand feet above sea level. They were able to rent a rambling twelve-room house called Villa Henriette which came equipped in good colonial style with a cook and two maids. His first three months were spent in and around Tananarive, where he found the higher colonial officials "uniformly courteous and helpful and in many cases really friendly." [13] But there was a "strong anti-American feeling." He attributed this to ill feeling over the settlement of the French debt for World War I. Both the French authorities and colonists and even the resident British started a rumor that he was a secret agent of the United States government sent to Madagascar to survey the island with an eye to its purchase by the United States.[14] He did discover that his cook had been bribed to

[13] RALPH LINTON, "Report on Work of Field Museum Expedition in Madagascar," *American Anthropologist*, 29, 1927, No. 3, p. 297.
[14] *Ibid.*, p. 298.

report weekly to the French administrator about the activities of his household. This seems to have caused him little trouble for he was well received in Tananarive by the Académie Malgache, a group of scholars who were carrying on research in several fields of study. In Tananarive he was able to study the collections in the local museum and "various rare books in the Government and Académie Malgache libraries" to acquire a knowledge of the language and the culture and to make a start on his collections for the Field Museum. He also took copious notes on the old Hova, the dominant tribe around the city, using old people and missionaries as informants.

In the next few months, Linton and his wife made short trips by railroad and motor car in the region around Tananarive, into the region of the Betsileo tribe, and to Lake Aloatra. During this period Linton contracted malaria, which developed into "black water fever," a serious disease which for a time seemed to make it desirable for him to leave the island. However, his health improved sufficiently for him to remain, although he continued to suffer frequent bouts of malaria during his entire stay in Madagascar and even after his return to the United States. Mrs. Linton also became ill in Madagascar. By this time Linton knew that he would have to travel widely over the large island—it is one thousand miles long and on the average 259 miles across. Transportation would be difficult and not suitable for a woman in poor health, so it was decided that Mrs. Linton would return to the United States to recuperate and to join her child.

So, in the middle of 1926, Linton began his travels throughout Madagascar by coastal boat, motor car, and by what would be called in Africa safari. He crossed the island twice and traveled from the far north to the extreme southeastern point at Fort Dauphine. In a report seemingly written from Madagascar and dated September 9, 1926, he had this to say about travel in Madagascar.

✠ *Outside these main lines, there are practically no roads over which one could use a wheeled vehicle, even a bullock cart. Horses, which might solve the problem, are unable to stand the climate. Even those imported from Africa soon die. All Europeans and rich natives travel in filanzana, a chair slung between two poles, which is carried by shifts of bearers. Eight to 12 men are required, as the* natives are accustomed to fast marches and light loads. Forty pounds per man is the legal load limit, and forty to forty-five kilometers a fair day's march. There are practically no volunteer bearers to be had at the present time. Men are obtained from the government, which exacts bearer service as a form of tax. The rate varies slightly from province to province, but is normally 4 fcs. per day without rice, with 2 fcs. per day for the return journey, making an actual price of 6 fcs. a day for time of travel. Bearers are usually changed at district headquarters, the old men going back to their own district. As they are forced labor, there is a great deal of grumbling and malingering, but desertions are rare and thefts from loads almost unknown.[15] ✤

Then, there was the problem of hospitality and accommodations. In this same report, Linton explains:

✤ Living conditions are fairly easy as compared to Central or South America or even the Pacific Islands. There are fairly good hotels in all the large ports and the capital, and indifferent ones in a very few of the largest interior towns. When traveling one stays at the village house. Each large village has one of these for the use of European travelers. It is the duty of the village chief to see that they are provided with food at reasonable price. Travelers carry their own beds, chairs, and cooking utensils, and are accompanied by a cook and a boy. Food is very cheap in the back districts, but there is no variety, the regular thing being chicken and rice, with a rare egg or banana. Stores in the larger towns carry a small line of canned goods, but bread is unobtainable outside the largest places. The chief is expected to provide fuel and water free of charge, but expects a tip.[16] ✤

One must remember that Ralph Linton was a big man, much larger than the average French administrator or colonist. He must have needed several teams of bearers. He did not have a very high

[15] *Ibid.*, p. 293–94.   [16] *Ibid.*, p. 294.

opinion of some of the tribal groups through whose territory he traveled. "The Betsimisaraka are stupid and lazy, and insolent unless kept in check," [17] he wrote. But on the other hand, "The Tsimahety are moderately straightforward and courageous, and are courteous to whites, but indifferent." [18] And,

> ✛ *The Sakalava are by far the bravest of the Madagascar tribes, and are also fairly intelligent. They are extremely proud, and are likely to be surly and insolent. They are well armed, and still cause the government considerable trouble. A lone white man traveling in the more remote parts of their territory is often denied food and lodging in their villages and annoyed in other ways. His life and property are usually safe. They hate the Merina much worse than they do the whites and frequently kill them. They are friendly toward Arabs, being partially Mohammedanized, and I am now trying to get an Arab interpreter to accompany me in their territory. They are rich in cattle and care little for trade, so I fear collecting (for the Museum) among them will prove difficult.* [19] ✛

Linton did not have an easy time of it during his penetrations into the interior of Madagascar. On one occasion he noted: "Unfortunately my best informant was suspected of poisoning me when I had a sharp attack of fever and was killed by the other natives, who were afraid of trouble with the government." [20] On another occasion his bearers became recalcitrant. He was warned that he might be poisoned and that members of their tribe were known as expert poisoners. He made a practice of having the cook serve all of his men first, then taking a plate from one of them at random to ensure that there was no poison in the food. He bought and traded for ethnographic objects throughout these trips; for example, among the Tsimihety, "Slightly over 250 objects were purchased or donated." [21] Furthermore, he took notes on social organizations, religion, and other facets of ethnography. Most of these notes have remained unpublished, but

[17] *Ibid.*, p. 296.   [18] *Ibid.*, p. 296.   [19] *Ibid.*, p. 297.
[20] *Ibid.*, p. 304.   [21] *Ibid.*, p. 305.

he did publish in *The Atlantic Monthly* several essays on his experience, one of which, "Witches of Andilamena," is included in this volume.

Linton's most intensive field research in Madagascar was among the northern Tanala, where he worked for over two months. The results of this research were published in his monograph *The Tanala: A Hill Tribe of Madagascar* (1933), and later formed the basis, along with his rather extensive notes on the neighboring Betsileo tribe, for his interpretative synthesis in *The Individual and His Society* by Abram Kardiner, a short portion of which appears in this volume. By the time Linton settled down for research with the Tanala he was well prepared by extensive experience in other regions of Madagascar. There are many common features in Malagasy tribal cultures. Linton selected the Tanala for special study because he felt that they represented a rather archaic stratum—a more equalitarian group without marked ranking and without social classes and slavery, which had developed among the Betsileo and the Merina, for example. Despite the short period of research, his monograph on the Tanala is thorough and replete with excellent ethnographic detail. It covered the standard categories of culture as seen by anthropologists at that time —economic life (including material culture), social organization, government, religion, weapons and warfare, amusements, art, life cycle of the individual, proverbs, a legend, and historical documents on the wars of the Tanala with the Hova and with the French.

Linton was particularly interested in Malagasy religion and magic, and his monograph is strong in details in this area. Among the Tanala, the medicine men or shamans were known by the generic term of *ombiasy*, of which there were several types. Among the Tanala-Menabe, Linton speaks of two main classes, the *ombiasy manangrata*, who were spiritualist mediums often marked by some slight nervous or mental abnormality, and the *ombiasy mpsikidy*, whose activities were concerned mainly with divination, the manufacture of charms, curing, and the like. This latter class was of two types, the *ombiasy ndolo* and the *ombiasy nkazo*. Both performed almost identical functions but each derived his magical functions from different sources. The *ombiasy ndolo* were under the control of one or more ghosts, usually ancestors. On the other hand, the *ombiasy nkazo* derived their powers from acquired knowledge. They were technicians who depended upon mechanical means of divination, knowledge of incantations, manufacture of charms and interpretation of the special days in the Tanala calendar.[22] Any intelligent man who could raise the fees necessary to pay a teacher could become an *ombiasy nkazo;* in fact, it was a way for frustrated younger sons to escape the domination of their fathers and older brothers. If an ambitious younger son lacked the fees for training he might work up a series of hysterical seizures, supposedly dictated by an ancestor ghost, and thus become an *ombiasy ndolo.*

Just as he had studied wood carving in the Marquesas, Linton hired an instructor to train him in the art of becoming an *ombiasy nkazo* among the Tanala. He had the funds to pay his teachers and he also had extra capital in the form of charms and divination procedures which he had collected on his travels among other Malagasy tribes. The Tanala *ombiasy*, eager to acquire new skills, were willing to trade in kind, charm for charm. One of the basic techniques which Linton had to learn was the form of divination called *sikidy*, which operates on somewhat the same principles as Arabic sand divination (the Tanala probably acquired it from Arabic peoples at some earlier time) or Greek geomancy. There are two forms, *big sikidy* and *little sikidy*, the former being a much more complicated system.

In *little sikidy* the diviner must have a receptacle containing about fifty seeds. Linton was told that the seeds must never be counted, for if the diviner knows the exact number he loses his power. The seeds are carried in a pouch or basket, but in the case of more opulent *ombiasy* they are housed in more elaborate containers. The two sets which Linton brought back with him and used in divination sessions were a lidded box of richly carved wood and an elaborately engraved brass receptacle. These were donated by Mrs. Linton to the Peabody Museum at Yale, along with the charts and directions for their use.

[22] RALPH LINTON, *The Tanala, a Hill Tribe of Madagascar*, Field Museum of Natural History, Anthropological Series 22, 1933, pp. 201–203.

Included with each set are two charms: a crystal and a piece of wood or horn. These are charms to summon the spirits which control the divination. The diviner must intone an incantation to call the spirits before laying out the seed pattern.

In the simpler form the diviner takes a random handful of seeds, which he then removes in groups of three, leaving a remainder of one, two or three. They are laid in position and the process is repeated until eight positions are laid out. He then places the crystal, which is a charm for clear-sightedness, below this row and proceeds to add eight more positions. He can now begin the complex interpretation. The number of seeds in each position is indicative: one representing weakness, two most favorable, and three a somewhat dangerous strength. The arrangement of pairs is significant and there is a different key position from which to interpret the pattern for a child, a virgin, a married person, an old person, and so on. Furthermore, the diviner must be familiar with the significance in the calendar of lucky and unlucky days. *Big sikidy* employs a larger number of seeds, which are taken away by twos rather than threes, and the pattern is much more intricate. *Sikidy* is able to predict only the near future; its range is about a year, the explanation for this being that the spirits can foresee the working out of present trends but not beyond that.

Linton became an expert at interpreting *sikidy* among the Tanala and continued to practice the art as a sort of parlor game on his return to the United States. However, this proved a rather embarrassing form of entertainment when *sikidy* predicted unpleasant things too accurately. On one occasion Linton performed a *sikidy* reading for Mrs. Eugene Davidson, the wife of the president of the Yale Press. He informed her that there were signs that one of her children would have an illness or an accident. While the guests were having cocktails after the reading, the phone rang and it was the Davidson's maid to inform the parents that their son had fallen out of a tree and broken his arm. After *sikidy* predicted the death of a close friend, who passed away four months later, and gave intimations of his own heart attack, Linton stopped using *sikidy* as a game. Linton's attitude toward the supernatural was always ambivalent. Although he was well grounded in science, he did not discount the idea that there could be elemental forces at work not measured by scientific techniques. While at Columbia he formed a close association with J. D. Rhine, who was just beginning his work in parapsychology at Duke University, and Linton followed his experiments in extrasensory perception with much interest.

As is the case with many anthropologists who have worked with primitive peoples who have a strong belief in the supernatural, Linton had a number of experiences with spirit phenomena which he could not dismiss as mere coincidence. One of these experiences in Madagascar occurred when he was traveling to a Betsileo village. The missionary for the village, whom Linton had met en route, expressed his regret that he would not be present during Linton's visit, but offered him the use of his house. The housekeeper would be there, however, to make Linton comfortable. Linton arrived in the village with an interpreter; he moved into the house, where his room and dinner were prepared. That night he worked late on his notes and went to bed, falling asleep immediately. Suddenly he was awakened by a jerking and shaking of the bed. He sat up, lit a lamp, and inspected the bed and the room. There was no one in the room nor were there wires or ropes attached to the bed. He decided that he had been dreaming. But as soon as he was asleep the same thing happened and the following night the same phenomenon occurred. He told his interpreter about the occurrences and the man laughed, saying: "I wondered how long it would take you to mention it. That housekeeper is a widow and wants to get married again. She planted a love charm in the room." The two searched the house examining the doorsills, the fireplace, and other places where charms could be placed but they found nothing. Linton called the housekeeper and solemnly informed her that he was married and that in his country a man could have but one wife. He warned her that unless she removed the charm he would report her to her missionary employer and she would lose her job. She protested innocence but from then on the bed remained stationary at night.

In the late fall of 1927 Linton left Madagascar, visiting Mozambique (Portuguese East Africa) and Rhodesia before sailing back through the Suez Canal to Europe. Some time after his return to

Chicago, the Field Museum announced plans for another expedition, this time to New Guinea, and asked Linton to undertake the assignment. The idea appealed greatly to Linton for he was eager to continue his studies of South Seas culture. The malaria which he had contracted in Madagascar continued to plague him; he was still having mild attacks of this malady in Illinois. And, one must remember that these were the times before the development of synthetic drugs against malaria. Only rather massive doses of quinine would suppress it and it often hung on for years even after a person had returned to a temperate climate. New Guinea was famous for its virulent strain of malignant malaria, and Linton's physician warned him that it would be suicidal for him to undertake an expedition to a malarial zone. This was a disappointment and also an embarrassment to a man who had always considered himself impervious to hardship or minor illness.

THE WISCONSIN YEARS

So, in 1928, Ralph Linton entered academic life after sixteen years as a field and museum anthropologist. He had never entertained any strong desire to teach. He found his life as a curator, explorer, and field researcher in archeology and ethnography highly satisfying. But at this time, when it was apparent that he could not return to tropical countries for some time, an offer from the University of Wisconsin to introduce anthropology as part of the curriculum in the Department of Sociology was very tempting. He accepted a position as Associate Professor in Anthropology and the next year he was promoted to full Professor. At Wisconsin he did not abandon field research. He spent several summers in archeological field work in the northern part of the state in cooperation with the Milwaukee Public Museum. In the summer of 1934 he was in charge of the Laboratory of Anthropology's field training trip to the Comanche Indians of Oklahoma. It was during these years at the University of Wisconsin, however, that Linton fully developed his talents both as a teacher and a theorist in cultural anthropology.

In spite of his initial reluctance to take up a teaching career, Linton was an immediate success in the classroom. He was a magnificent and dramatic lecturer. He used to say that to lecture successfully to undergraduates one had to be part ham actor and part priest. This he was able to achieve, for with a fund of stories and amusing examples drawn from his field experiences, he was always entertaining on the platform. With his sincere enthusiasm for his subject, his fluent command of language, and his depth of understanding, he could also be inspiring. Linton believed with Emerson that the duty of an educator was to make hard things easy. His lectures seemed to the listener to be spontaneous and informal but they were in fact carefully thought out. Linton never wrote his lectures but he invariably made an outline on cards which he carried with him but often did not refer to while speaking.

The short piece which came to be titled "100 Percent American," and which has been reprinted more often than anything Linton ever wrote, came about in response to a question by a student at the end of a lecture on diffusion. In an ad lib reply, Linton used the example of a man getting up in the morning.

✤ Our solid American citizen . . . throws back covers made from cotton domesticated in India and wool from sheep domesticated in the Near East. . . . He slips into moccasins, invented by the Indians of the Eastern Woodlands, and goes to the bathroom, whose fixtures are a mixture of European and American inventions. . . . He takes off his pajamas, a garment invented in India, and washes with soap invented by the ancient Gauls. He then shaves, a masochistic rite which seems to have been derived from either Sumer or ancient Egypt. ✤

The account goes on in this fashion, taking man through dressing and eating breakfast, and then:

✤ When our friend has finished eating he settles back to smoke, an American Indian habit, consuming a plant domesticated in Brazil, in either a pipe derived from the Indians of Virginia, or a cigarette derived from Mexico. . . . While smoking he reads the news of the day, imprinted in characters invented by the ancient

Semites upon a material invented in China by a process invented in Germany. As he absorbs the accounts of foreign troubles he will, if he is a good conservative citizen, thank a Hebrew deity in an Indo-European language that he is 100 percent American.[23] ✣

The students who were privileged to hear this ad lib "bit of anti-quarian virtuosity," as Linton called it, rose to their feet and gave their professor the traditional Wisconsin "Sky rocket." This was the first time this had occurred in his classes and he confessed that it was somewhat disconcerting at the start, for the cheer begins with a long drawn out hiss, followed by "Boom! Ahh! Whee! Linton!" Since this formulation proved so successful, Linton included it later in *The Study of Man;* he expanded it somewhat for the *American Mercury* at their request, from whence it was picked by the *Reader's Digest.* It was later included in numerous anthologies both here and abroad.

As a teacher, he was much more than an outstanding lecturer to undergraduates. He was able to establish with his own students that sort of relationship which he himself had never achieved with his professors. He was informal and made young people feel at ease. At Wisconsin between 1928 and 1935 he acquired a considerable following of serious students, many of whom he directed into graduate studies at other universities, since Wisconsin did not as yet offer a graduate degree in anthropology. Among those students who began their anthropology with Linton are John Gillin, Sol Tax, Lauriston Sharp, Clyde Kluckhohn, and E. Adamson Hoebel.

Linton made a strong impression on students, often stronger than he himself was aware. He was able to listen and he made himself available to students with problems, either personal or academic. He hated to lunch alone, so would frequently invite a student to join him. This might be followed by an hour or more of discussing the student's difficulties. But when he encountered the student again he might fail to place him or remember his name. A typical example is remembered by his wife. One evening he handed her a letter he had received from a young graduate student at another university.

[23] RALPH LINTON, *The Study of Man, an Introduction,* New York, Appleton-Century, 1936, pp. 236–37.

The writer said that the lunch she had had with Dr. Linton changed her whole life. After their discussion, she wrote, she had revised her entire dissertation, which had subsequently been approved for the Ph.D. and accepted for commercial publication as well. On the strength of this work she had been offered a fine job. "That's very interesting," said Linton's wife, "who is the girl and what did you tell her?" "You know," confessed Linton, "I can't remember a thing about it and I haven't the foggiest idea who she is." However, he was not always so vague, for he enjoyed a life-long friendship with many of his former students.

For a time Linton was the only anthropologist at Wisconsin. Later, Dr. Charlotte Gower joined him in the Department of Sociology and Anthropology to share his ever-increasing teaching obligations. In a joint department, and at a university where the social sciences were developing, Linton established contact with colleagues in other departments, and these contacts with other disciplines marked a turning point in his intellectual approach to his own subject. He mentions particularly E. A. Ross, a sociologist of considerable reputation, and Kimball Young, a well-known social psychologist, as being particularly helpful in their respective fields. Clark Hull, Harry Harlow, and Abraham Maslow stimulated his interests in individual personality development. He also profited from long conversations with John Gaus, a political scientist, and with the philosophers, F. C. Sharp and Eliseo Vivas. It should be noted that Maslow and Vivas were then graduate students and young instructors; both later became leaders in their respective disciplines.

Furthermore, while Linton was on the faculty at Wisconsin, an experimental college was established on the campus by the well-known educator and philosopher, Alexander Meikeljohn. This college concentrated on the problems of order and change in the civilizations of classical Greece and their relevance to the modern world. The students were also encouraged to read widely in the social sciences and especially in cultural anthropology. The discussions of the nature and the organization of culture and civilization in classical Greece, using the tools of contemporary social science, produced concepts new to the classroom and enlightening for the teachers as well as the students. Although Linton did not teach in this dynamic but short-lived experimental program (it lasted from 1927 to 1932), he participated in many planning sessions and discussions. From such colleagues and from participation in interdisciplinary programs Linton's horizons were broadened beyond the historical anthropology in which he had been trained. He became increasingly aware of the many problems which could best be studied through the collaboration of several disciplines, and familiarized himself with the modern concepts of social psychology and sociology. The former field worker and museum-oriented anthropologist was becoming a social scientist with wide interests in many dimensions of human behavior.

Since Linton was rather isolated from other anthropologists, he continued to maintain informal contacts with Chicago colleagues whom he had known during his tenure at the Field Museum. In 1931 A. R. Radcliffe-Brown came to Chicago University as Professor of Anthropology. Radcliffe-Brown was, at that time, the leader of the British structural-functionalist school of anthropology, a distinction which he shared somewhat reluctantly with Bronislaw Malinowski. Radcliffe-Brown soon gathered about him at Chicago a group of disciples, Ralph Linton met Radcliffe-Brown several times in Chicago. Radcliffe-Brown introduced Linton to the functional approach and changed his thinking, just as he influenced Robert Redfield, Fred Eggan, Sol Tax, and others.

Radcliffe-Brown himself was swayed by French sociology, particularly the work of Émile Durkheim. He was in fact a comparative sociologist working with the data of primitive society. He was explicitly searching for sociocultural laws through the comparative study of social structures which he conceived as being the core of any society. He conceived of function "as the total set of reactions that a single social activity or usage or belief has to the total social system." [24] Thus, Radcliffe-Brown saw each society as an inter-related system which formed a structure (actually he used an organism analogy) in which each part was functionally related to the total. He was critical of the use of history by anthropologists, since primitive

[24] A. R. RADCLIFFE-BROWN, *A Natural Science of Society*, Glencoe, Free Press, 1948, p. 85.

38

societies lack historical records, and critical of the historically oriented American anthropologists. Thus, he advocated synchronic analysis or studies on one time period. Marvin Harris, in his book *The Rise of Anthropological Theory*,[25] has done a masterly job of analyzing the background, the successes, the changes, and the modifications of British "social anthropology"; and he has stressed Radcliffe-Brown's role in this movement within anthropology.

Linton's encounters with Radcliffe-Brown in Chicago are said to have resulted in some lively and heated discussion, the heat more on Linton's side since Radcliffe-Brown was self-assured and arbitrary in his pronouncements. He was also older and more firmly established in his profession. Linton, as always, reacted adversely to any form of authoritarianism. Linton disliked Radcliffe-Brown as a person, although he respected and assimilated many of his ideas. In some ways the two men were similar. Both were brilliant lecturers and conversationalists and both had the ability to stir and inspire students, although Radcliffe-Brown at Chicago and later at Oxford was more inclined to acquire disciples. Linton was more willing to listen and to accept new ideas, while Radcliffe-Brown, even in 1931, made no concessions to viewpoints that conflicted with his own.

Personal animosity, however, did not prevent the two men from offering a joint seminar session at the University of Wisconsin in 1936. Radcliffe-Brown came to Wisconsin University accompanied by a collection of his devoted followers, and the session turned into a confrontation and was one of the most stimulating events that Wisconsin social sciences had produced. The two men provided quite a contrast on the rostrum: Radcliffe-Brown, tall and arrogant in beautifully tailored English clothes, a monocle, and a long cigarette holder; Linton, big and burly in rumpled unmatched tweeds and smoking a pipe. Linton did not attack Radcliffe-Brown's functional theories in total, but he did reject his rather arbitrary formulations of so-called structural-functional laws as not being based upon empirical fact but upon intuitive speculation. Furthermore, Linton, both by training and personal inclination, disliked the imposition of any

[25] MARVIN HARRIS, *The Rise of Anthropological Theory*, New York, Thomas Y. Crowell Co., 1968, pp. 514–67.

elaborate theoretical system such as that Radcliffe-Brown was trying to achieve. He also felt that Radcliffe-Brown in his sociological search for "laws" was ignoring the biological and the psychological reality of man. Linton did not, however, disdain the most important elements of Radcliffe-Brown's functionalism, namely, the insistence upon detailed field studies and the anaysis of each society as an interrelated system. In fact, it can be said that Linton became a functionalist, although differing in many basic concepts from the functionalism of Radcliffe-Brown and of Malinowski, with whom he shared many ideas and with whom he was later closely associated.

In 1936, while still teaching at the University of Wisconsin, Linton published *The Study of Man*, which represents his basic anthropological theories and position and is considered today his most important work. This book seems to have been at first written as a text for an introductory course in anthropology, and follows in general his basic course offered at the University of Wisconsin. In his preface he states: "This book has been largely inspired by the difficulties which the author encountered in his search for some work which was broad enough in its scope to provide beginners with a grounding in the essentials of Anthropology." It was written in a simple, direct, and easy-flowing style, an effect which Linton worked hard to produce. He had little patience with social science jargon and the scholarly obfuscation of many academic writers. The book has little of the framework of a textbook; there are no chapter subdivisions, and there is only one footnote, no list of "further readings," and a sketchy bibliography. It was totally unlike other textbooks of the time such as Alfred Kroeber's *Anthropology*. The book received scant attention when it first appeared and it was never reviewed at all in the *American Anthropologist*.

The Study of Man soon began to receive attention, not only as a text, but among scholars for its originality and the clarity of its theoretical position. The book begins traditionally enough with a discussion of fossil man and race which was adequate for the epoch; it includes late chapters on discovery and invention, diffusion of culture traits, historical reconstruction, and cultural classifications which were standard subject matter for anthropology of the time. To each of these traditional interests of anthropology, Linton, however, provided a precise synthesis and original new insight. His careful analysis of the many variables involved in diffusion, which he saw as a combination of three distinct processes—namely the presentation of a new culture element or elements, the acceptance by the receiving society, and the integration of the new element into the pre-existing culture— was a much-needed corrective to the rather automatic concept of diffusion held by such members of the culture area school as Leslie Spier, Clark Wissler, and others.

In *The Study of Man* Linton provides a reconciliation of functionalism with a historical approach to culture and, above all, he provides precise tools of analysis. His functionalism is closer to that of Bronislaw Malinowski than to that of Radcliffe-Brown; he sees the social and cultural system as a response to biological, psychological, and social needs of man. A culture is made up of *items, traits, complexes,* and *activities.* The type of string used in a bow, for example, is an *item;* the bow itself which has a string, a kind of wood, a shape, and size is a *trait;* the bow is part of a larger unit of culture consisting of the bow, arrow, quiver, and other associated traits which form a *trait complex.* In turn, the trait complex focusing upon the bow and arrow is part of a major *activity* which may be the securing of food through hunting or self-defense in warfare.

It is on the level of the trait complex that function becomes evident. The bow-and-arrow complex may provide at the same time several functions, namely food getting, defensive or aggressive war, or even recreation. Thus the function of a given trait complex may be different in different cultures and its function may change in time. He uses the example of fencing in our own culture: in medieval times it was necessary for self-defense but in modern times it is but a sport.

Another set of concepts in this book helps unite functionalism with a historical approach to culture. Each element of a culture (that is, an item, trait, trait complex, or activity) has four qualities, namely a *form,* a *meaning,* a *use,* and a *function.* The *form* of a trait complex includes those aspects which can be directly observed—the physical as well as the overt behavioral aspects. The *meanings* of the trait complex are covert, consisting of the associations which a society attaches to a trait complex which are sometimes subjective and unconscious. The distinction between *use* and *function* is not so clearcut. Linton defined *use* as "an expression of its (i.e. culture element) relation to things external to the social-cultural configuration" and "function is an expression of its relation to things within the configuration." [26] He draws the distinction more clearly by citing an example of what he had in mind: "the use of medicine may be to reduce fever, its function is to restore individuals to health. The function of a trait complex is the sum total of its contribution toward perpetuation of the social-cultural configuration." [27]

These distinct qualities of trait complexes are useful in understanding culture growth and diffusion. Obviously in the transfer of a trait complex from one sociocultural system to another it is the form that is most easily comprehended. The meaning is often changed in the new context and provided with new associations, and the use and function of the trait complex may even be modified. Sometimes traits which are independent in one sociocultural system become trait complexes in another simply because they derive from the same source. An amusing example of this sometimes used by Linton in the classroom is that of five-gallon gasoline tins, dresses, and the Bible in Polynesia. When Christian missionaries arrived, they brought all three—gasoline tins, dresses, and the Bible. The tins were immediately accepted as magnificent water containers; these prized objects were given to those who accepted the Bible and thus also garbed themselves in the modest Mother Hubbard dresses. A more serious example of the independence of these qualities is that of the Sun Dance among the tribes of the Great Plains. It was found in a whole series of tribes with only slight differences in form but varied strikingly from tribe to tribe in meaning, use, and function. In one it was the fulfillment of a vow, in others it ensured the revenge of a relative, in others it was a way of seeking a guardian spirit, and in another a test of the powers of a new medicine man.[28]

[26] *The Study of Man, an Introduction*, New York, Appleton-Century, 1936, p. 404.
[27] *Ibid.*, p. 404.   [28] *Ibid.*, p. 405.

Furthermore, these qualities of trait complexes show their independence in time. Form seems to have the greatest stability; all of us are aware of the conservative aspect of such overt ritual as a marriage ceremony long after the meaning, the use, and even the function has been modified. We are also aware of new trait complexes that arise to fulfill the use and the function of an older trait complex. Thus the horse and carriage complex disappeared upon the appearance of motor vehicles to provide transportation and communications. It survives only in such limited locales as Central Park in New York City and a few other places where the horse and carriage is a recreative form of transportation for romantics. "Clearly, the value of functional studies," said Linton, "can be increased by taking these additional factors into consideration and especially by a refinement of techniques which will make it possible to deal with them adequately." [29] He demanded that functionalism be concerned with the dynamics of culture. As he stated: "the instant that the investigator tries to deal wih the dynamics of culture or to establish laws in the more commonly accepted usage of the term, he finds himself dealing with factors which operate in the field of time." [30] Linton in *The Study of Man* brought history into a functional approach and provided concepts which appreciably sharpened functional analysis.

Still, it is in the chapters of *The Study of Man* concerned with the analysis of particular societies that Linton made the greatest impact upon anthropology and sociology. In these chapters he presents a well-defined concept of a social system. Central to his concept of a social system and its internal consistency and relationship to the individual is his concept of status and role. This concept, especially as it was elaborated by Linton, has had an important influence on social anthropology, sociology, and social psychology. He put forward this concept first in *The Study of Man* [31] and extended his thinking on the subject in his later book *The Cultural Background of Personality* [32] and in several articles.

---

[29] *Ibid.*, p. 420.   [30] *Ibid.*   [31] *Ibid.*, pp. 113–31.
[32] RALPH LINTON, *The Cultural Background of Personality*, New York, Appleton-Century, 1945, pp. 76ff.

In essence, the concept was not entirely new to sociology. The concept of role, in a sense a theatrical analogy, "has been central to those sociological analyses which seek to link the functioning order with the characteristics and behavior of the individuals who make it up." [33] Sociologists had used the term for the expected behavior of individuals in recurring situations in a society. Robert Park, George H. Mead, and others had made use of "role theory," and Jacob Moreno had made role enactment a basis for psychotherapy method. However, it seems to have been Ralph Linton who defined "role theory" most precisely and added to it a new dimension. For Linton, individuals within any society occupy a series of positions which he called statuses. This concept of status should not be confused with the hierarchical ranking of people—that is, a high or low status or a legal status. In Linton's sense status is a place or a position that an individual occupies in a social system—a father, a butcher, a neighbor, a member of a professional association, an employee, a young man, and literally hundreds of other positions. Some of these statuses are *universals*, common to all or most members of any society, and some are *specialized*, occupied by only a small segment. Some status-positions are *ascribed* at birth, such as one's sex, race, membership in an Indian caste or in a family unit. Others are *achieved*, that is, acquired in one's lifetime through learning or by another method, such as wealth, success in warfare, and the like.

For each status, there is a role which Linton spoke of as the "dynamic aspect" of status. The role is what a person in a given status is expected to do, and each culture defines what role is expected of a person in a given status. In all cultures, for example, there is the status of "father," but the role of father is defined differently in different cultures. At first, there was some confusion among Linton's readers as to whether he thought of the role as a normative pattern of behavior or the actual behavior of a person in a given status. He later made this clear by speaking of *ideal culture patterns*, that is, how a person in a given status ought to behave in a given situation as against *real culture patterns*, that is, how a people in a

[33] RALPH H. TURNER, "Role: Sociological Aspects," in *Encyclopedia of Social Sciences*, 1968, Vol. 13, p. 552.

given status actually do behave.[34] Linton realized that the degree of consensus as to what are "ideal patterns" as well as the conformity of people in any society to such "ideal patterns" varied from society to society and from time to time. He warned against confusing the real behavior in a society and the construct which the anthropologist develops from the statements of his informants and his observations of modal behavior. Thus, he introduced the terms *culture construct* and *total culture construct* for the abstract picture which the anthropologist presents of a society and its culture.

❖ *In order to present a comprehensive picture of any culture or to manipulate culture data, the investigator has to develop a culture construct. He establishes the mode of the finite series of variations which are included within each of the real culture patterns and then uses this mode as a symbol for the real culture pattern. Thus if the investigator finds that the members of a particular society are in the habit of going to bed sometime between eight and ten o'clock but that the mode for his series of cases falls at quarter-past nine, he will say that going to bed at quarter-past nine is one of their culture patterns. Such a modal derivation may be termed a culture construct pattern.*[35] ❖

Yet these same people may claim that eight o'clock is proper bedtime (ideal pattern). The *total culture construct pattern* is a series of modal behavior patterns which combine all of the culture constructs of a given society. At the heart of this theory is the concept of status and role; any given role may have an ideal pattern and a real pattern of behavior for any situation. They are the key to the development of the culture construct for the anthropologist.

Every individual in any society has a series of status-positions; a man may at the same time be a member of a secret society, a father, an uncle, and a son-in-law, a member of a generation or age set, almost *ad infinitum*. In one situation the individual acts out the role of a father, in another that of an employee, and in another that of a

[34] RALPH LINTON, *The Cultural Background of Personality*, p. 43.
[35] *Ibid.*, pp. 45–56.

member of a secret society, and so on. Seldom does an individual act in accordance with but one status-role but rather as, for example, a middle-class (status-role is middle class) father (kinship status-role). Likewise, any status-role is always defined vis-à-vis another status-role. A father behaves differently as the father of a daughter than as the father of a son. Robert Merton, refining Linton's status-role concepts, spoke of status sets and role sets,[36] that is to say, a set of related statuses to which a set of related roles are attached; thus a man who is a professor of anthropology must necessarily have status-role relations vis-à-vis students, deans and other administrators, departmental colleagues, publishers, and assorted colleagues in the American Anthropological Association. Finally, a refinement of Linton's earlier concept is that of status sequences; our same professor of anthropology most certainly requires that over a period of time he or she was an undergraduate, then a graduate student, maybe a teaching assistant, a field researcher, and so on.

Linton himself refined these concepts both in *The Cultural Background of Personality* and in several articles, one of which is reprinted in this volume, indicating the usefulness of the concept in studies of personality and culture. He indicates in this article that what could be called status-role sets on the normative level may influence personality structure. There is (or at least there used to be) a picture in our heads of the personality of a college professor—mild, forgetful, tweedy in attire, bookish, apt to be oblivious of his role as a father or husband, and not practical in economic matters. Likewise, we have a composite picture of the personality of a butcher. Some individuals tend to conform to such stereotype status-role personalities but others present personality traits inconsistent with their status-role. Thus, several years ago in an excellent movie called *Marty* Ernest Borgnine portrayed the character of an ugly but highly sensitive and romantic butcher—an inconsistent set of personality characteristics in terms of his status-role sets. The concept of status-role has become an important analytical instrument which has been used far beyond the confines of anthropology. Neal Gross and his associates, for example,

[36] ROBERT MERTON, "Continuities in the Theory of Reference Groups," in *Social Theory and Social Structure*, Glencoe, 2nd ed., 1959.

have not only provided us with an excellent critique of "role theory" but they have also made use of these concepts in a study of the status-role of the school superintendent in the United States.[87]

With his concept of status-role, Linton provides a basis for relating the individual to his society and its cultural system which has become basic in the thinking of many social scientists.

COLUMBIA UNIVERSITY AND NEW YORK

The Study of Man, despite its initial neglect, brought Linton into the anthropological limelight. Without doubt, it was this book that earned him the invitation to join the faculty of Columbia University. In 1936, the same year that the book was published, Franz Boas retired from Columbia University after teaching there for thirty-seven years. In these years, Boas dominated American anthropology through his research, teaching, and writing. He had made Columbia the center of American anthropology, and his students, such as Alfred Kroeber, Robert Lowie, Paul Radin, Edward Sapir, and a host of others, were the leaders of anthropological thought in the United States. It was Boas who selected the President of the American Ethnological Society, and the same almost might have been true of the President and other officials of the American Anthropological Association. He administered the Anthropology Department at Columbia with a paternalistic but authoritarian rule. In his later years, he was commonly referred to as "Papa Franz." But he viewed his department in European terms—as a "cathedra" of which he alone was the professor. In 1936 only Boas among the anthropologists at Columbia had tenure.

With his tremendous prestige and his divergent views, he frequently clashed with the university administration, which was headed by the autocratic Nicholas Murray Butler. Obviously Boas intended to appoint his own successor and to see to it that the Department of Anthropology at Columbia continued to be administered as it had been under his leadership. The university administration, however, had other ideas. An ad hoc committee was appointed to study the Department of Anthropology and to recommend appointments in

[87] NEAL GROSS, *et al., Explorations in Role Analysis,* John Wiley, New York, 1958.

that field. Robert McIver, the well-known sociologist, was a member of that committee, and he was well-versed in the trends of anthropology both in the United States and abroad. This committee undertook a search. It is not known exactly which men were discussed, although it was rumored at the time that Radcliffe-Brown and W. Lloyd Warner were considered. It is a fact that Boas's former students were passed over. In 1937 Ralph Linton was invited to Columbia University as visiting Professor of Anthropology; William Duncan Strong, a Berkeley-trained archeologist, came from the Smithsonian Institution as Associate Professor of Anthropology; and George Herzog, who had studied at Yale University and who specialized in linguistics and comparative musicology, was made Assistant Professor of Anthropology. It was more or less understood that, if mutually agreeable, Ralph Linton would be Senior Professor and Departmental Chairman.

Linton's first months at Columbia University were difficult ones. When he went to pay his respects to Boas the old man's greeting was, "Of course, you know this was not what I wanted." Boas, as Professor Emeritus, continued to occupy two offices, one for himself and one for his secretary and research assistants. The outside entrance to the second office had been blocked by bookcases. Since "Papa Franz" could not be disturbed, Linton was assigned the adjoining office through which the assistants had to pass in going back and forth to their own office.

Ruth Benedict was then an Assistant Professor without tenure and was that year acting Chairman of the Department. Linton's previous encounters with Benedict at meetings and conferences had been cordial and he had looked forward to working with her. Her own book, *Patterns of Culture*, had appeared just two years earlier and Linton had been much impressed with this delightfully written and stimulating book. Although he did not from the first agree with her characterizations of cultures as wholes, he was eager to discuss her theories. However, Benedict was cool and unreceptive to Linton as a colleague. It was rumored that Benedict was Boas's own choice for his successor. Without tenure and as a woman (there were no women in the graduate faculties at Columbia at that time), she undoubtedly felt challenged by Linton's appointment. Benedict, with several years of graduate teaching behind her, had a devoted following of students who expressed their loyalty by snubbing Linton. It was reported that a petition was sent to the university administration requesting that Linton not be given a permanent post as he was a poor teacher and an inferior scholar.[38] The administration took care of this by giving Linton his permanent appointment in November instead of waiting until April, as was the usual custom.

Unlike Linton, who directly professed his likes and dislikes, Ruth Benedict had an irritating manner of regally dismissing the ideas and accomplishments of those whom she did not hold in high regard. She would not openly criticize, but with a smile or a gesture indicate that she felt her adversary to be elementary or childish. Linton found such treatment infuriating and frustrating, and the relationship between the two colleagues developed into intellectual and personal hostility, sustained more in after years on his part than on hers. While Linton's attitude toward people tended to be frank and friendly, once he came to believe that a person was working against him he became supsicious and resentful. He continued to be quite implacable in his feelings toward Benedict until her death in 1948. However, each maintained considerable dignity. They were able to attend faculty meetings together and to examine doctoral candidates without outward signs of hostility. It was possible for a graduate student to study with both and to be friendly with both, although there was an underlying narrow line that anyone had to walk if one wanted to work with both.

In his first two years at Columbia Linton attracted a group of graduate students, many of whom had been studying with Ruth Benedict, Alexander Lesser, Gene Weltfish, and others. Graduate students at Columbia University soon discovered that Linton had much to offer. One of his first major endeavors was to organize a seminar on acculturation, to seek funds to send graduate students to

[38] IF SUCH a petition was actually sent, it is not in the Columbia University files. Frank Fackenthal, who was then Provost of Columbia and later its acting President, once told Charles Wagley that he had destroyed several derogatory documents pertaining to the Linton-Benedict feud.

the field, and to edit a volume, *Acculturation in Seven American Indian Tribes*,[39] in which the field research of several graduate students and recent Ph.D.s appeared; and in this same volume two final chapters developed his own thinking about the phenomena of acculturation, which was a central subject in American cultural anthropology at that time. Excerpts from the final chapters of this book are included in this volume.

Boas had refused to teach in Columbia College (it is said that he had a disagreement with Dean Herbert Hawks over the giving of grades at mid-term to undergraduates) although he would teach undergraduate courses in Barnard College, the women's college affiliated with Columbia. Linton, however, offered an introductory course in anthropology in Columbia College which soon became very popular.

In his mid-forties Linton was a vigorous and imposing figure. He was over six feet tall and weighed well over two hundred pounds. He was fond of food, being both a gourmet and a gourmand at table. Music, dancing, cards, and alcohol had not been permitted in his home and he never developed any interest in the first three. But he overcame the last taboo and enjoyed the conviviality of pre-dinner cocktails as well as after-dinner highballs. He was, however, always a moderate and purely social drinker. He dressed well, if rather informally. Highly articulate in discussion, he was a first-rate raconteur with a fund of stories gleaned from his experiences in the field. His students and colleagues alike were appreciative of what they learned from him during out-of-class bull sessions. He had a habit of trying out new theories by thinking aloud with students and friends, developing his ideas for anyone to share as they took form in his mind. By no means a stolid professor or a timid scholar, he read widely and most retentively, mostly in his own and related fields but he liked to relax with science fiction, serving for a time as advisor to a pulp magazine of this genre. He was a colorful and creative personality who would have been an outstanding figure on any campus.

Just previous to his move to Columbia, Ralph Linton had served on a subcommittee of the Committee on Personality and Culture of the Social Science Research Council with Robert Redfield and Mel-

[39] New York, Appleton-Century, 1940.

ville Herskovits. This subcommittee functioned from 1935 until 1938. In 1936, in the *American Anthropologist*, these three anthropologists collaborated on and published their now famous "Memorandum for the Study of Acculturation," which was used by a whole generation of students of anthropology to frame hypotheses for field research and for analysis of field data. At Columbia Linton found a group of young anthropologists who had been doing field research among American Indian tribes under a project financed by the Council on Social Science Research of Columbia University. During the summer of 1937, through the Department and from the Works Progress Administration (WPA), funds were raised to send several more individuals into the field.[40] Some of the work was directly oriented to acculturation as defined in the Herskovits, Linton, and Redfield "memorandum"; some earlier field work reported in this volume was analyzed in accordance with this frame of reference. There are long articles by Marian W. Smith on the Puyallup of Washington State; by Jack S. Harris on the White Knife Shoshoni; by Marvin K. Opler on the Southern Ute; by Henry Elkin on the Northern Arapaho; by Natalie F. Joffee on the Fox Indians of Iowa; by Iriving Goldman on the Alkacho Carrier of British Columbia; and by William Whitman on the San Idelfonso Pueblo of New Mexico. Some of these papers were doctoral dissertations at Columbia.

Linton's own contribution to the volume, "The Process of Culture Transfer" and "The Distinctive Aspects of Acculturation" (see pp. 125–51 of this volume), are two carefully thought out essays on the process of culture contact, diffusion, and acculturation. Some of his thinking derives from his collaboration with Redfield and Herskovits, but it can be readily seen that he had developed his own concepts. There is little in common with Redfield's thought as presented in *The Folk Culture of Yucatan* nor with Herskovits's views on the modification and persistence of African culture in the New World. While Redfield was interested in the use of a folk-urban continuum developed by studies of four contemporary communities in Yucatan

---

[40] IT MUST be remembered that these were years of the Great Depression. Graduate students drew funds from NYA (National Youth Administration) and professional anthropologists worked for the Writers Project of WPA.

to the neglect of history, Herskovits was primarily historically inclined, combining a historical with an ethnographical approach to
communities of Negroes in the New World. Linton, on the other
hand, was interested in the process of the transfer of a culture element
from one society to another—its presentation, acceptability to the
recipient society, its reintegration and modification, and its effect
upon the total sociocultural configuration. Today, one may have
serious doubts that acculturation can be thought of as a distinctive
aspect of culture change, although it has become a standard word in
social-science vocabulary. Linton's analysis of the process of culture
change through culture contact, through diffusion, and through even
selective or directed change stands as a classic study of the process of
culture growth and sociocultural change.

As an offshoot of his thinking about acculturation, Ralph Linton
found the funds to send two other Columbia students to the field
armed with hypotheses on the acculturation process. At first, he had
planned to undertake acculturation studies in Madagascar, where he
was fully aware of field problems. In order to train potential field
workers, he offered in 1938 a semester course on the cultures of
Madagascar, but it soon became apparent that a European war was
imminent and that Madagascar as a French colony might not be
opened to field research. So, with the funds available for acculturation
studies, Linton selected Charles Wagley to undertake field research
in a central Brazilian Indian tribe and Carl Withers to work in a
small American town. Neither of these research projects resulted in
the kind of acculturation research for which Linton had provided
hypotheses, but each did result in published material. Wagley was to
have studied the results of acculturation during the first ten years
or so after a primitive people had first entered into contact with
Western culture, as well as the influence of individuals in the acceptance and rejection of culture traits and elements. The Tapirapé
tribe seemed from all reports to be an ideal laboratory for such a
study. He found, however, that depopulation from European diseases
had arrived before Western culture and had seriously modified the
social structure and that there were no "continuous first-hand contacts" between the Tapirapé and Brazilians. Withers was to have

studied the effects of the many New Deal reforms on a small farm community. In a sense, he came near to his goal, for his well-known book *Plainville, U.S.A.*, written under the pseudonym of James West, does attempt in part to do just that. The book's greatest value, however, lies in its analysis of the social structure of a small midwestern town and its problems just before World War II.

Linton was not upset that neither of the field workers had followed through faithfully in testing the various hypotheses on acculturation with which he provided them. He was himself eclectic and fully aware of the influence of field conditions upon the outcome of field research and of the common anthropological necessity to modify hypotheses to fit the field situation. Besides, by 1940, when the field workers had returned to New York, Ralph Linton was fully involved in another interest, namely personality and culture. This was not a new interest for him. He had devoted a chapter to the subject in *The Study of Man*, and much of his theory in that book was concerned with the relationship of the individual to his society and culture. In the late 1930s, however, personality and culture was the major focus of interest in anthropology at Columbia and at various other centers in New York. This was due primarily to the influence of Ruth Benedict, whose book *Patterns of Culture* had characterized cultures by conceptual types, the controlled and subdued Appolonian-type and the more overt, orgiastic, and open Dionysian-type. Each culture was more amenable or receptive to different individual personalities and tended thus to produce personalities consistent with the particular culture. Margaret Mead was not teaching at Columbia at the time, but through her relationship to Benedict and Boas, she had considerable influence upon graduate students. Her work in Samoa, the Admiralty Islands, and New Guinea is well known. Also teaching at Columbia in those days was Otto Klineberg, already a nationally known social psychologist, who was almost as well trained in anthropology as in psychology.

From 1935 to 1938 a series of seminars were held at the New York Psychoanalytic Institute on anthropology and psychoanalysis under the direction of Abram Kardiner, a practicing analyst. In these seminars various cultures were "presented" (that is, described and analyzed) by anthropologists and their data interpreted by psychologists. Cora DuBois presented the Trobriand, the Kwakuitl, and the Chuckchee cultures based, of course, upon the written work of Malinowski, Boas, and Bogoras, respectively. Ruth Bunzel and Ruth Benedict presented the Zuni based upon their own extenisve field research and earlier writing on the Pueblo culture. Finally, Ralph Linton was asked to present the Marquesan and the Tanala cultures.

> ⬦ It was not until the Tanala and the Marquesan cultures were studied that we found we could make an attempt to survey cultures as a whole. This was due to two factors: our technique in the form of working concepts had become sufficiently accurate to permit such application, and Dr. Linton's descriptions were sufficiently complete to permit us to see aspects and relationships which in the presentation of previous cultures could only vaguely be conjectured.[41] ⬦

This statement is both a tribute to Linton's descriptive ability and to his prodigious memory and a serious admission as to the weakness of the basic data upon which the concept of the basic personality type was created. Linton himself frequently expressed regret that he did not have a better knowledge of psychology when he did his own field work, but his thorough knowledge of the two cultures made him a valuable collaborator. It must be remembered that Marquesan culture was practically destroyed when he did research on it, and that the period he spent with the Tanala was short. He did not have biographies or autobiographies or psychological tests; and he had not seen a full-year cycle of life in the latter community. He was, however, a sensitive observer with a fabulous hindsight memory.

In any case, Abram Kardiner postulated the concept of basic or modal personality mainly from such data. Linton defined the concept succinctly as

> ⬦ that personality configuration which is shared by the bulk of a society's members as a result of early experience which they share

[41] ABRAM KARDINER, in Author's Preface, pp. xxiii–xxiv, to *The Individual and His Society*, New York, Columbia University Press, 1939.

in common. It does not correspond to the total personality of the individual, but rather to the projective system, or in different phraseology, the value systems which are basic to the individual's personality configurations. Thus, the same basic personality types may be reflected in many different forms of behavior and may enter into many different personality configurations.[42] ❖

Kardiner postulated two types of cultural institutions, namely *primary institutions* focused upon the family, which are such aspects as infant feeding, toilet training, sexual training and taboos, family organization, subsistence techniques, and the like. Such *primary institutions* are "older, more stable, and less likely to be intefered with by vicissitudes of climate or economy." [43] These are the institutions most directly at work in forming the basic personality of the society. In turn, it is the basic personality which expresses itself in the *secondary institutions* such as ideology, myth, religion, and the like. Knowing the primary institutions, one can predict the basic personality type and knowing the basic personality type one can predict the nature of, but not the content of, the secondary institutions. These concepts seemed to be valid in the cases of the Tanala and the Marquesas but Kardiner himself admitted that he could not account for primary institutions without the aid of history. "All we know about them is that there is a limited number of possibilities in the attempt to satisfy cerain biological needs of man." [44]

In 1940 the Kardiner-Linton seminar was transferred to Columbia and became a regular course in the curriculum of the Department of Anthropology. A new series of cultures were presented and analyzed, such as the Comanche by Linton, that of *Plainville, U.S.A.* by Carl Withers, the Tapirapé by Charles Wagley, and Alor by Cora DuBois. Cora DuBois had been a participant in this work from its very inception. In addition to her outstanding work in cultural anthropology, she had acquired training in psychology and in administering such

---

[42] RALPH LINTON, Foreword, p. viii, to Abram Kardiner, *The Psychological Frontiers of Society*, New York, Columbia University Press, 1945.
[43] ABRAM KARDINER, *The Individual and his Society*, p. 471.
[44] *Ibid.*, p. 471.

psychological tests as the Rorschach, TAT, and the like. In 1937 she had set out for Alor in the Dutch Indies to carry out a study which would test the psychodynamic scheme that had come from the analysis of hindsight descriptions by anthropologists. She returned in 1939 with Rorschach protocols, children's drawings, eight extensive life histories, and more important, a thoroughgoing knowledge of a living society and culture. Kardiner, with the help of DuBois and Linton, used the ethnographic data to construct the Alorese basic personality. The Rorschach and children's drawings were given to Emile Oberholzer for independent analyses. Their conclusions turned out to be strikingly similar—the Alorese were insecure, suspicious, indifferent, and full of apathy. Such personality characteristics were related to Alorese childhood, during which mothers neglected their children for long hours spent in gardening. Cora DuBois published her own findings in *The People of Alor* (1944), but later she published a chapter in *Psychological Frontiers of Society* (1945), edited by Kardiner, in which descriptions and analyses of *Plainville, U.S.A.* by James West (Carl Withers) and of the Comanche by Linton appeared.

The Kardiner-Linton collaboration was certainly a "breakthrough" for the epoch in the study of personality and culture. It seemed to be generally verifiable by field research, but there were many disagreements between Abram Kardiner and Ralph Linton and the other anthropological participants in the seminars. Kardiner was not an anthropologist and he learned slowly. After he had propounded his primary institution—basic personality—secondary institution scheme, he constantly defended his concepts; sometimes, it seemed to Linton and to other anthropologists, to the distortion of ethnographic data and established anthropological theory. There was considerable bickering and occasional flareups. Kardiner dismissed one cultural analysis because the ethnographic data was inconsistent and weakly reported in the field of child training. There was an argument over the presence of the so-called toothed vagina myth in one culture. This myth tells of supernatural women who entice men into intercourse but who have vaginas armed with teeth. He, of course, saw profound psychological significance in the myth (which, of course, it does have) but he could not understand that the myth was almost universal in the region. It was not a central story in the mythology of the people in question nor could he find anything in the child training or other primary institutions that indicated any special fear of women by men. Furthermore, Ralph Linton and the other anthropologists rather resented being used as "informants"; both books represented collaboration between Kardiner and Linton; yet the theoretical sections appeared under Kardiner's name with contributions by anthropologists. Such bickering led to the assigning of the royalties of *The Psychological Frontiers of Society* to the Department of Anthropology of Columbia University rather than to any of the authors.[45]

Linton accepted the validity of the basic personality concept and, to a certain extent, the projective system which Kardiner postulated as arising from early childhood experience. Early experience established in the individual what Kardiner called a "projective system," which in its simplest terms means that throughout life the individual tends to interpret new situations in terms of their real or assumed similarity to his childhood experiences and to have at first an unintellectualized response based on this experience. In the Proceedings of the Interdisciplinary Conference held under the auspices of the Viking Fund, November 7–9, 1947, Linton said:

❖ *The modal personality for any society can be established directly and objectively by the study of the frequencies of various personality configurations among the societies' members. . . . There can be no question that these frequencies do differ markedly from one society to another. A configuration which must be considered normal for one society on purely statistical grounds may be highly aberrant for another. The modal personality for any society corresponds to the statistical established norm.*[46] ❖

(See pp. 151–59 in this volume.) It must be noted that Linton used "modal" rather than "basic" to describe the personality type and that

[45] Full royalties were stored to Abram Kardiner upon the publication of the paperback edition.
[46] S. S. SARGENT and Marian W. Smith, eds., *Personality and Culture*, Viking Fund, 1949, p. 163.

he implies that one arrives at this personality type by a different route than by analysis of the so-called primary institutions. And, in his Foreword to the [first] hard-cover edition of *The Psychological Frontiers of Society*, Linton wrote

> ✤ *Kardiner's investigation had dealt primarily with the effects of particular projective systems upon the development and perpetuation of particular institutions. My own interest had been in the relation of culture to personality content and in the adaptation of individuals to particular positions within the social system.*[47] ✤

Linton's Foreword was not included in the paperback edition of the same book.

During these first years of research on personality and culture, Linton seems to have been reluctant to put his own ideas on the subject, independent of those of Kardiner, on paper. He was working to clarify and organize his point of view and he made his ideas known in lectures and in discussions with colleagues and students. In February of 1943 he was invited by his alma mater, Swarthmore College, to give a series of five lectures on the general subject of inter-relations of Culture, Society, and the Individual. These lectures were sponsored by the Cooper Foundation and were to be open to townspeople as well as students and faculty. He mentions the pleasure of renewing his acquaintance during the course of these lectures with Dr. Harold C. Goddard and Dr. Samuel Palmer, who had been his teachers in his undergraduate days. As usual, Linton lectured from notes; however, it was customary, he learned, for the lectures to be published at the end of the series with a subsidy from the Cooper Foundation. This posed a problem for Linton. Although he lectured easily and informally, he was, as we have said, a perfectionist in writing. He did not wish his first publication on personality and culture, which was highly important to him, to appear as a group of semipopular lectures. So, he was forced to write and in doing so he became seriously involved in putting forth the theories and concepts which he had been

[47] ABRAM KARDINER, *The Psychological Frontiers of Society*, New York, Columbia University Press, 1945.

mulling over for so long. Except for the chapter headings, the book which emerged, *The Cultural Background of Personality* (1945) is said to be quite unlike the lectures. Because of the need to compress the subject matter into five chapters (five lectures), it is brief and compact. Although written with Linton's usual lucidity and simple terminology, there is little space for clarifying examples and each sentence is loaded with theoretical import.

The book was not published by the Cooper Foundation. After he had delivered the manuscript, he went to see the youthful editor of the Swarthmore-Cooper Foundation series, who informed Linton that the manuscript was not suitable as presented, that it was confusing and too difficult. The young man obviously was unfamiliar with the subject matter. "If that is your judgment, I think that the Foundation should be released from publication," said Linton. He knew that the book would have little circulation and that any royalties would accrue to Swarthmore College should it sell at all. When the young editor agreed, Linton joyfully scooped up the manuscript and hurried to the offices of Appleton-Century, who had published *The Study of Man* and had been after him for another book. This book, now in paperback, is still used widely in teaching and read by scholars in several disciplines in the social sciences.

More than any other publication on the subject, *The Cultural Background of Personality* reveals Ralph Linton's view of personality and culture. It refines his concepts of status and role and his ideas regarding the participation of the individual in his society and culture which were first presented in *The Study of Man.* The essay on status personality included in this book reveals the differences between the approaches of Linton and Kardiner to personality and culture. In this essay, he mentions the basic personality concept and seems not to doubt its validity, but he presents the formation of the personality almost entirely in structural-functional terms. It is in this book that he introduces his "Status Personalities." These are, as stated earlier, response configurations linked to status positions and they are different for men, for women, for children, and so on; in stratified societies, similar differences in status personalities may be expected of nobles, commoners, and slaves. "The status personalities," he wrote, "recognized by any society are superimposed upon its basic personality type and are thoroughly integrated with the latter. However, they differ from the basic personality type in being heavily weighted on the side of specific overt responses." [48] Thus, status personalities are not at odds with the basic personality type of a society, but they are more specific and they are responses which can hardly be directly related to what Kardiner called primary institutions. How can one learn to behave as a grandfather from early childhood training? It is only after the individual becomes aware of the expected model of a grandfather that specific behavioral responses of that status personality may be acquired.

Linton's approach to the relationship of personality and culture is more concrete and specific; and less dependent upon the vagaries of neo-Freudianism than that of the psychoanalysts. It is also more dynamic, for sociocultural systems do change; new technological-environmental arrangements create new status positions and status personalities for which early childhood training makes no preparation. With the appearance of new status personalities, although molded by earlier value orientations, do not the primary institutions of a culture change? In his contrast between the dry and wet rice producing Tanala, Linton found basic clues for Tanala personality structure. We would agree with Marvin Harris that the crucial flaw in Kardiner's basic personality scheme lies in its lack of diachronic dimension for changes in the basic organization of a sociocultural system which creates new needs and tensions. Linton's concept of the status personality provided a tool for injecting change into what would be a homeostatic condition.[49]

When the United States entered World War II, the normal academic and research activities of most anthropologists were interrupted. Ruth Benedict went off to Washington to undertake studies "at a distance" for the Office of War Information. William Duncan Strong

[48] RALPH LINTON, *The Cultural Background of Personality*, New York, Appleton-Century, 1945, p. 130.
[49] MARVIN HARRIS, *The Rise of Anthropological Theory*, New York, Thomas Y. Crowell Co., 1968, pp. 438–41.

became the head of an organization called the Ethnogeographic Board which provided basic data to the Armed Forces. Other anthropologists worked with the Office of Strategic Services both in Washington and in the field. Linton felt strongly about this war, and was eager to become part of the war effort, not this time in a spirit of adventure, but because he felt so strongly about the horrors of the Nazi regime. For a time he thought that he might be sent to Madagascar with a British expedition. He spent considerable time in Washington as a consultant on Madagascar, but finally the British Government decided against any American involvement in this project. At forty-eight years of age and with a background of tropical disease, he could hardly enlist: so he continued to teach his classes at Columbia, although enrollment at this time was meager. He also journeyed to New Haven once a week to conduct classes at Yale. The department there was seriously understaffed, as G. P. Murdock, John Whiting, and C. S. Ford were all working for the U.S. Navy in New York. But it was at Columbia during the war years that Linton found a role in the war effort—and one that added a new dimension to his anthropological career.

In 1942 Professor Schuyler Wallace, who was Chairman of the Department of Public Law and Government (now Political Science), formed at Columbia a School of Military Government and Administration for the U.S. Navy. Linton became involved in the new school from its very inception. The purpose of the school was to train naval officers for the duties of military government in different parts of the world. Its curriculum included courses in various languages, history, government, and the ethnography of various regions of the world. The Navy was particularly interested in the Pacific for obvious reasons. For equally obvious reasons, anthropology was discovered to have considerable practical value for the Navy, which was faced with Melanesia, Micronesia, southeast Asia, and south Asia as zones of combat and probable future administration. Linton taught classes on Micronesia, Melanesia, and Polynesia. G. P. Murdock and John Whiting were brought to Columbia as naval officers to add to the staff, and anthropologically trained linguists taught unwritten languages through informant techniques.

This school, and others like it which were formed at American universities, demonstrated the value of anthropology in practical situations. This became an important preoccupation of anthropologists in the rather idealistic period following World War II when anthropologists were able to do research toward the reconstruction of peace. Much of the research begun at Columbia during the war continued after the war in detail-studies of Micronesia aimed at intelligent and peaceful administration and development of the island cultures. And, Margaret Mead and Ruth Benedict could continue their "studies at a distance" for peace and world reconstruction with funds from the U.S. Navy. In any case, the war experience with regional studies convinced Columbia University of the need for a School of International Affairs based to a large extent upon the Naval School. This was the genesis of the School of International Affairs and the several related Area Institutes which were formed after World War II. It was this war, and our national unpreparedness in the understanding of exotic cultures, which prepared the ground for the era of so-called Area Studies which followed.

Linton's experience in these war efforts made him especially sensitive to the contribution of anthropology to international studies and affairs. Thus, in 1945 he edited a book, *The Science of Man in the World Crisis*,[50] which brought together a group of articles by outstanding anthropologists and other social scientists who wrote papers on the application of their particular field of interest to world problems. This book contained articles on the concept of culture, on demography, biological anthropology, psychology and anthropology, and other subjects of current interest. It was a landmark, so to speak, in applied anthropology, yet each author surveyed his field of interest in an objective manner.

His war experience also taught Linton the fact that North Americans were ignorant of the non-Western cultures of the world and convinced him that we must learn. Again, he brought together a group of scholars knowledgeable about non-Western areas, persuading them to write rather comprehensive articles for a book which he called

[50] RALPH LINTON, ed., *The Science of Man in the World Crisis*, New York, Columbia University Press, 1945.

62

Most of the World.[51] In this book were papers on Africa, Japan, India, and most of the under developed areas of the world. His raison d'être for this book was succinctly stated in his Introduction:

❖ *The renewed clash in Europe and the battle with Japan have given subject peoples their chances, and the last semblance of European hegemony is disappearing as the Asiatic colonies break away one by one and the various "spheres of influence" reject the policies of their former guardians. Although some of the feebler or less advanced groups may be kept in colonial status for a few generations longer, it is obvious that the colonial system is on its way out.*[52] ❖

This is a prophetic statement, but little did he know that even the "feeble and less advanced groups" would demand their independence so rapidly. His effort and foresight again were a very early and basic contribution to regional studies which for a time became a central focus of education in the United States. He was a man of his time, able and willing to turn his interests to the crucial problems of the epoch.

In the spring of 1945, Linton went to South America on a grant from the Viking Fund, a new foundation dedicated to anthropology which became known subsequently as the Wenner Gren Foundation. He had met Paul Fejos, the foundation's director, and had acted as his close adviser in setting up the program of the foundation. Fejos had a special interest in South America, having carried out his own first ethnographic research among the Yagua Indians of the upper Amazon. Linton's trip was to be both a survey for the Viking Fund and, it was hoped, a much-needed vacation. He had been teaching at Columbia, at Yale, and in the Naval Administration School, the latter a year-round operation with no time off in the summer. However, Linton's vacations were seldom relaxing. He was a bull of a man who thought that he had the energy to do anything he needed or wanted

[51] RALPH LINTON, ed., *Most of the World*, New York, Columbia University Press, 1949.
[52] *Ibid.*, p. 8.

to do. He had friends, former students, and colleagues in South America in government service who were specialists in South American anthropology. He had never been to South America before, so in his survey-vacation he tried to see as much as possible and to talk with many social scientists.

He spent most of his time in Peru and Brazil. In Peru he was more or less in the expert hands of Harry Tschopik, an advanced graduate student from Harvard University who had carried out extensive ethnographic field research in the highlands of Bolivia and Peru. After about two weeks in Lima, where Linton visited museums and talked with many people, Linton and Tschopik took off for Cuzco, the ancient Inca capital situated over 12,000 feet above sea level in the Andes. It was a rough trip by automobile and, at that time, the accommodations en route were rather primitive. Linton arrived in Cuzco exhausted and feeling rather odd. He was assured that it was but a mild case of *siroche*, or altitude sickness, which many people coming into the highlands felt. It would disappear in a day, he was advised. Linton made a practice of ignoring minor illness: he would go about his regular business with a temperature of 102° when he was suffering from recurring bouts of malaria. So, the next morning after arriving in Cuzco he traveled to the ruins of Machu Picchu. At that time, Machu Picchu could be approached from Cuzco by rail, but to reach the ruins themselves one had to climb over two thousand feet from the Valley of the Urubamba River along a steep path. It is not known whether he climbed afoot or rode one of the donkeys which could be rented. In any case, once he was within the ruins of the abandoned city, climbing about again was the only way to see it.

When he arrived in Rio de Janeiro, some days later, he complained of not feeling well but did not interrupt his plans, keeping up a busy schedule both social and anthropological. At the National Museum, he went painstakingly through the ethnographic collections and was enchanted to find a Hawaiian feather cloak which had been given to the Brazilian Emperor, Dom Pedro II, in the nineteenth century. He helped Dr. Heloisa Alberto Torres, who was then the director of the museum, to identify numerous objects of material culture. Linton's fame as an anthropologist had spread to Brazil, and he gave a lecture to a large audience at the Faculty of Philosophy of the University of Brazil sponsored by Professor Artur Ramos. He spoke in English with simultaneous translations into Portuguese furnished by Charles Wagley. After this lecture, one bilingual member of the audience said that both lectures were excellent but that they were not the same. What Wagley had said was more of an interpretation of Linton's lecture than a translation of it.

From Rio de Janeiro, Linton traveled up the coast of Brazil by plane. He stayed several days in Belem at the mouth of the Amazon River where the famous Emilio Goeldi Museum is located. In Belem he was "off loaded" for lack of a war-time air travel priority. Belem was a hub of the war effort, a U.S. Air Force base from which wild rubber from the Amazon was being shipped by air. By 1945 the flow of human and air cargo was to the United States rather than to Belem. Linton might have waited days, even weeks, to board a commercial plane. But Wagley's colleagues in the U.S.-Brazilian health service came to his rescue. They secured a place for one passenger on a plane operated by the Rubber Development Corporation for freight and occasional passengers. Linton thought it strange that they asked him not to accompany them to the corporation office to seek the passage, but he understood when he arrived for the take-off. Linton weighed then approximately 240 pounds. He had been eating well in Rio de Janeiro, where beef was plentiful and cheap during the war. The pilot had calculated on "an average 175-pound man" and since the DC 3s left Belem carrying an absolute full load some recalculation of freight had to be done. So Linton arrived in Miami listed as "freight essential to the war effort" resting on the cold bucket seat of a drafty DC 3.

He did not feel at his best, of course, when he arrived in New York, but all the doctors could advise was a rest. In December he attended the annual meetings of the American Anthropological Association in Philadelphia, at which he was elected President. That evening he suffered extreme chest pains. The hotel doctor called it indigestion caused by late hours, the excitement of the meetings, and the banquet. He returned to New York, stayed in bed for a couple of days, and then tried to attend a few Christmas parties. Finally, he went to his doctor, who read his cardiogram and discovered that he had indeed suffered a coronary occlusion. He took the next semester off from teaching but he was soon back to his very active life. His heart condition slowed him down somewhat, but despite symptoms of angina he would merely stop what he was doing for a minute or two, take a nitroglycerin pill, and then charge ahead, not following closely any regime prescribed by the doctors. He did stop smoking; and to keep his hands busy, he took up needle-point work, using designs from primitive art which he remembered. But he exasperated his wife, his doctors, and his friends by continuing a schedule of activity that would have exhausted a younger and healthier man.

STERLING PROFESSOR AT YALE UNIVERSITY

In 1946 Ralph Linton was invited to become a Sterling Professor of Anthropology at Yale University. These were (and still are) highly prestigious and well-paid positions in the academic community. Linton had many friends in the Anthropology Department at Yale, some of whom he had worked with during the war. He also reasoned that New Haven would be a less hectic community in which to live and work; thus, living there would be better for his health. Columbia did everything possible to persuade him to remain but even his colleagues there had to agree that maybe some distance between Linton and New York might be best for him. So he moved to New Haven, buying a large house on Willow Street with a finished third floor where a graduate student might live. Floyd Lounsbury was its occupant for a time. Linton found the working conditions at Yale excellent— research and secretarial assistance, and interesting and cooperative colleagues. But the idea that some distance from New York might slow down his pace turned out to be wrong. He was soon lecturing to large undergraduate classes, taking part in extra seminars, and now traveling frequently from New Haven to New York to keep up his old interests and to see old friends and colleagues.

One of the reasons that he traveled so frequently to New York was his interest in primitive art. His work as a collector for museums had allowed him to further his collecting bent, and he long made a practice of seeking out antique and curio shops wherever he went, looking for non-European objects of aesthetic interest. He bought carvings, textiles, bronzes, ceramics of Oriental, Polynesian, African, or American Indian design. He had a special sensitivity and knowledge of material culture. It was said of Linton that he never forgot an object, describing it, telling where it came from, and even placing it in a particular case in a particular museum. Art objects were both a visual and emotional experience for him. Thus, in the early 1950s he was a frequent and valuable guest on a television program sponsored by the University of Pennsylvania Museum called "What in the World." On this program various ethnographic specimens from the museum storerooms were presented to a panel of experts for identification. Where did it come from? What period (if it was an archeological speciment)? What was it used for? Linton was seldom stumped and was more often correct than many highly trained specialists in a given area of the world or a specific archeological period.

Linton's art expertise was not limited to the non-European field, although that was his central interest. Kal Kelemen, the art historian, tells of an incident which much impressed him. It was Linton's first visit to Kelemen's home. As the two men were talking, Linton picked up an enameled ash tray from the table beside his chair and casually examined it. "Where did you get this" he asked. "I bought it in Lima, Peru," answered Kelemen. "The design is Peruvian," Linton said, "but it can't be Peruvian workmanship. It looks like Wiener Werkestatte." "You are quite right," replied Kelemen. "It's Austrian art nouveau and I bought it from a Viennese refugee in Lima." Kelemen said that Linton had the most discriminating eye of any anthropologist he had known and better than that of most art historians.

Linton had had a strong interest in primitive art ever since his studies with Hopuani in the Marquesas had given him an insight into the abstract and symbolic conventions of form and design. By attempting to reproduce these he had learned to appreciate the skill and sophistication of the artist's abstractions which, unlike European abstract art, were not a mystifying expression of the artist's subconscious emotions but a conceptualization completely understood by all members of the society. Also his work in the Field Museum had given him an opportunity to study the art forms of many cultures. At Columbia Linton came to know Paul Wingert of the Art History Department who was in the process of setting up a course in primitive art. Later the two men collaborated on the Museum of Modern Art's show called Arts of the South Seas, and Linton, Wingert, and René d'Harnoncourt wrote the catalogue for that show. Linton was also a consultant and collaborator for the show of the Arts of the American Indian at the Museum.

After he went to Yale, Linton refined his aesthetic interests and became a serious and devoted collector of African art. Genuine old pieces, made in the ritualistic fashion and not for the tourist trade, had already become quite rare, for between the missionaries who encouraged the Christianized natives to burn their masks and fetishes and the early European collections which had picked off many of the best pieces, there was little left even in Africa. When the Nigerian government decided to set up a museum of their own art, they had to come to New York dealers for much of their display. Linton had a few pieces which he had collected himself in Africa but most of his African art was purchased on Madison Avenue and 57th Street, where he combed the few galleries which offered primitive art in those days, seeking out the authentic and aesthetically valid pieces from among the fakes and those of inferior workmanship. Although African art has now become fashionable, at that time African art collectors were a small and select fraternity, all of whom knew one another and delighted in meeting to display and discuss their prizes.

Linton often came to New York with a suitcase containing a piece or two of African art seeking a trade for a better piece. Often it was two pieces for one, or one object plus an additional sum in dollars for another. He became known as a knowledgeable African art collector and wherever he went other African art collectors would seek him out: Webster Plass in London; Edward G. Robinson and Vincent Price on the West Coast; and in New York, Helena Rubenstein, Eliot Elisofon, and René d'Harnancourt of the Museum of Modern Art, who collected for Nelson Rockefeller. Soon Linton found himself indulging in a millionaire's hobby on a professor's salary, which made for some stress and strain. But he did succeed in acquiring a fine collection of over two hundred pieces which represented some of the very best aesthetic examples from many different tribes. A show of his collection of African art was planned by the Yale University Art Gallery for the spring of 1954. He had the satisfaction of knowing that his collection was to receive recognition at Yale but he did not live to see the exhibition itself for he died in December of 1953 before the exhibit took place in March. The collection was later purchased in its entirety and presented to the Yale Gallery by Mr. and Mrs. James Osborne. This would have delighted Linton, for the collection had more meaning intact than it would as scattered objects in various museums. Part of the collection is now on permanent display at the Yale Gallery and the remainder is on shelves in a storeroom where it can be studied by scholars with special permission.

At Yale, primitive art was not Ralph Linton's only, or perhaps we should say, his major interest. In fact, it was more of a hobby, for he never taught a course on the subject of primitive art. His interest in personality and culture persisted, and he held joint seminars on psychology and anthropology at the Institute of Human Relations, where a tradition had already been established for interdisciplinary research. In these seminars, he collaborated with Eric Fromm and later with Edward Stainbrook from psychiatry and with George P. Murdock, Clellan S. Ford, and John Whiting in anthropology. Some of Linton's further thinking in this field which developed out of his collaborative seminars at Yale appears in *Culture and Mental Disorders*,[53] a result of the Salmon lectures, which was edited after Linton's death by George Devereux. He became interested in the comparative study of deviants and psychotics, citing for example, Edward Stainbrook's research in Bahia (Brazil) of patients in a public mental hospital. This study was a direct offshoot from the Yale seminars in personality and culture. And John Whiting, who it must be said was already interested in personality and culture before Linton came to Yale, carried some of the Kardiner-Linton hypotheses into cross-cultural and statistical analysis using data from the cross-cultural

[53] RALPH LINTON, *Culture and Mental Disorders*, George Devereux, ed., Springfield, Illinois, C. C. Thomas, 1956.

files which became the Human Relations Area Files already established at Yale under George P. Murdock. These files contain data extracted from published sources of a sample of world cultures codified by topics (that is, child training).

Linton was not in his later years as active in culture and personality studies but he never lost his sense of their importance. In a concluding lecture of his undergraduate course, which was tape recorded and printed intact in his posthumously published book *The Tree of Culture*,[54] he had this to say:

❖ Some of the most important advances that are being made at the present time are, I believe, coming from the studies of personality and culture. For the first time we are beginning to get some insight into what human nature really is an how it is shaped. So that while adjusting forms to the machine at one end, we are more and more learning how we may operate to adjust human beings to this system at the other end.[55] ❖

At Yale University, Linton returned to an old interest which he had never really abandoned, the growth and development of world culture. His general course at Columbia had become each year more and more historical and broader in its coverage of world ethnography. At Yale, he added to his data as he expanded his knowledge. This course, in its earlier Columbia form and especially as it developed at Yale, was not for the average undergraduate, although with his easy delivery and fund of exemplifying stories Linton was able to hold the interest of even average undergraduates. It is doubtful whether any other anthropologist in the world could offer a course so broad in scope unless it was Alfred A. Kroeber, and he lacked Linton's classroom showmanship. In 1948 the Wenner Gren Foundation provided funds to have this lecture course transcribed and for several years Linton devoted his "spare time salvaged from a busy life" writing a book based upon these lectures, and using the transcriptions only as a guide and outline in writing. It was about two thirds completed

[54] RALPH LINTON, *The Tree of Culture*, New York, Alfred A. Knopf, 1955.
[55] *Ibid.*, p. 673.

in December of 1953 when he died. The transcriptions thus proved invaluable to Adelin Linton, who was able to complete the book, which was published in 1955 as *The Tree of Culture*.[56]

As Adelin Linton states in her preface,

❖ *The title of the book, refers, not to the familiar evolutionary tree with a single trunk and spreading branches, but to the banyan tree of the tropics. The branches of the banyan tree cross and fuse and send down adventitious, aerial roots which turn into supporting trunks. Although the banyan tree spreads and grows until it becomes a miniature jungle, it remains a single plant and its various branches are traceable to the parent plant. So cultural evolution, in spite of diffusion and borrowing and divergent development, can be traced to its prehistoric origins.[57]* ❖

Thus, *The Tree of Culture* is a study of cultural evolution, but not in the sense of unilineal nineteenth-century evolutionism nor even in the sense of stages of V. Gordon Childe or the culturological evolution of Leslie White. In this profoundly historical work Linton is concerned with the growth of culture through diffusion, migration, invention, innovation, reintegration, and adaptation. He was very much aware of cultural ecology in its limiting and creative effects upon the growth of culture, and his concept of diffusion, which he had earlier developed in his discussions of acculturation, is a far cry from a mechanical borrowing of traits of one culture by another.

The bulk of *The Tree of Culture* is devoted to the growth of culture in the Old World—the Eurasian continent, Africa, Japan, and the South Seas. The independent development of culture in the New World is treated more briefly, perhaps because this was one of the portions left unfinished by Linton. But the New World provides numerous parallels to cultural evolution in the Old World and the differences, such as the lack of the wheel and fewer and less useful

[56] An abridged version of *The Tree of Culture* is available in paperback (Vintage Books, Alfred A. Knopf, 1958).
[57] *Ibid.*, p. v.

domesticated animals, provide useful variables for his concepts of cultural growth.

In the Old World, Linton saw two main areas of cultural stimulation where man was able through the domestication of plants and animals to adopt sedentary village life and ultimately to build complex civilizations. One was the Middle East, where neolithic villages were established supported by the growing of grains and the use of the oxen as a traction animal and sometimes for food; the other was southeast Asia, where in the lowlands root crops such as yams along with taro and bananas and in the highlands, rice and yams, provided the basis for a similar type of sedentary village life. But as each of these two basic complexes spread, they received new elements from outside (such as the horse from the central Asian plateau), and mutually influenced one another. Divergent forms of society and culture appeared, adapted to local environmental and external conditions.

The Tree of Culture is almost impossible to present in digest, not only because of its enormous scope, but also because of the particular merging of various anthropological and historical methods and its subfields. Linton uses in this book his knowledge of archeology, of history, of the process of acculturation and diffusion, of functional analysis, and of the relationship of the individual to his society and to culture. The book is full of insights and hypotheses. For example, if anyone wants a bird's-eye view of the complexities of southeast Asian culture, the chapter on the "Southeast Asian Post Neolithic" (pp. 207–34) is recommended and relevant for today. An example of a very wide hypotheses is this statement: "The Classical civilizations have cast a spell over European scholars, yet one must admit that modern mechanized civilization of Europe owes more to the Northern European culture and their barbarian background than it does to either Greece or Rome." [58] This is not an H. G. Wells *Outline of History* but a theory-filled book. It would require analysis by specialists in many fields to be able to judge the substantive materials which it presents. To date there have not been any serious criticisms from such specialists regarding Linton's treatment of their special periods

[58] *Ibid.*, p. 256.

and areas of the world. This is a book that has brought together over forty years of research and thinking in various fields of anthropology.

RALPH LINTON: IN RETROSPECT

Ralph Linton died of a heart attack on Christmas Eve, 1953. He had led an exciting and full life but at the time of his death he was planning new lectures, articles, and books—and perhaps planning to acquire a new piece of African art he had spotted. In the last two or three years of his life, he had grown a beard, then still a symbol of dignified age. It was white and full and gave him the appearance of a patriarch, reminding one of Ernest Hemingway in his later years. But Linton did not feel like or act like a patriarch. His striking appearance, his worldwide fame as an anthropologist, and his ability to present a complex subject in terms understandable to a nonprofessional audience meant that he was more and more called upon for lectures and for conferences. Linton responded to the general public and they responded to him.

He was in no way a politically oriented man. In fact, he seldom discussed current politics as such, but he did have strong faith in liberal democratic institutions. He had a long-term conviction that the social sciences, particularly anthropology, could and should have an important role in dealing with social problems. Although he contributed fundamentally to the basic theory and substance of anthropology as a science, he often thought of himself as an interpreter or a synthesist of anthropology for a large audience. For example, in the preface to *The Study of Man* he mentioned as one purpose of the book: "It is wise for any science to pause from time to time and sum up what it has already accomplished, the problems that are perceived but still unsolved, and the inadequacies of its current techniques. The author has provided such a summary." [59] Yet with his professed interest in the relevance of anthropology to social ills and for the formation of public policy, he did not participate in the subfield of his discipline called "Applied Anthropology." Beginning in the 1930s, anthropologists such as Elliot Chapple, Fred W. Richardson, Conrad

[59] RALPH LINTON, *The Study of Man*, 1936, p. viii.

Arensberg, and others began to undertake research in factories, on coal mining towns, in problems of nutrition, and the like; and after World War II, anthropologists moved into public health, land reform, urban studies, and a broad spectrum of applied research. It was an age of optimistic idealism when the United States Government, UNESCO, ILO, and the U.N. itself, as well as a hundred other public and private agencies, called upon anthropologists for research and advice on how to introduce new technology, new customs, and how to modify peacefully forms of community organization. Except for one short paper, the result of a lecture, called, "An Anthropologist Views Point IV," [60] Linton did not participate in this type of anthropological research.

It was not that he was uninterested in applied anthropology nor unconcerned with the problems they tackled. Nor did Linton suffer from the ethical dilemmas which have come to bother anthropologists today when they are asked to provide information and put their skills to work for various agencies. Rather, Linton was always concerned with the basic theories of his science and the long-term view of human history. Much of his thinking about human society did provide tools for researchers in applied anthropology. His concepts of acculturation, his theories of status and role, and his views on personality and culture became basic instruments used by anthropologists working on social problems and policy.

He believed strongly that anthropology and the other social sciences could become rigorous and objective sciences, and he directed his efforts toward that end. Yet, throughout his work there is a humanistic tendency. He did not see man as an automatom reacting without any free will to the demands of his society and culture. He believed in the creativeness of the individual and of each society within the framework of its culture. Yet there was a certain pessimism about Linton's view of human history which several of his colleagues and former students have noted. He felt that he lived in a "rare period of freedom, one which could not last and which was already threat-

[60] In *American Perspective* (Spring 1950), pp. 113–21. Washington, D. C. Foundation for Foreign Affairs.

ened by bigotries which had appeared abroad and at home in his own lifetime." [61] In 1936, in the concluding paragraph of *The Study of Man*, he wrote,

✤ *The signs are plain that this era of freedom is also drawing to a close, and there can be little doubt that the study of culture and society will be the first victim of the new order. The totalitarian state has no place for it. In fact, for men to take an interest in such matters is in itself a criticism of the existing order, an indication that they doubt its perfection. Unless all history is at fault, the social scientist will go the way of the Greek philosopher.* ✤

He dedicated this book to "The Next Civilization." And, almost two decades later he concluded *The Tree of Culture* in the same vein, expressing the hope that the social sciences would use this period of unusual freedom to prepare some "solid platform from which the workers of the next civilization might go on." [62] One can only hope that Ralph Linton was wrong in his pessimism.

Although Linton became one of the world's most distinguished anthropologists, he never fitted the mold of the academic scholar and researcher. One of his drawbacks from the point of view on the contemporary anthropologist was his almost total neglect of the usual apparatus of scholarship. We have already mentioned that *The Study of Man* contained but one footnote and no references, which is true of practically all of Linton's articles and books, including the monumental *Tree of Culture*.[63] This practice does make his writing easier to read but it is frustrating to the serious student. Science should be accumulative; and time and time again, one wonders what precise school of thought Linton had in mind in his discussions of society and culture and one would like to be able to turn back to the original source when Linton has uncovered a surprising set of facts.

[61] Cf. LAURISTON SHARP, "Ralph Linton," in *Encyclopedia of the Social Sciences*, Vol. 9, p. 390 (New York, 1968).
[62] *Ibid.*, p. 390.
[63] *The Tree of Culture* does have a bibliography for each chapter but no specific references in the text.

One of the reasons why Linton dispensed with references was that he did regard himself as an interpreter or synthesist. He did not consider that he was writing only for the specialist. Another reason must have been his almost "freak" memory and his way of learning. He read prodigiously all of his life but, after graduate school, he seldom visited libraries or took notes as he read. When he heard of a book he wanted to read, he bought it and perused it at leisure. He seldom referred to the book again. He had a mind like a computer which filed away the facts and ideas that claimed his attention and he could reproduce this material at will, often verbatim. In fact, he remembered what he read so accurately that he used to worry when writing that he might reproduce something word for word and be accused of plagiarism, although he frequently had no recollection of where he had acquired the information. Had he read it in some book or had he acquired it from conversation with colleagues? Although he liked to talk, he could also be attentive and retentive as a listener. He had a gift for acquiring from discussion the information he needed to fill the gaps in his own knowledge and for filing it away with the same accuracy which he retained from the printed page, although again he usually forgot with whom he had the discussion. He always held that the best way to get information on a particular subject was to invite the man who knew most about it to lunch.[64]

❖ *Despite his reluctance to put references down on paper, it was rare that Linton could be "caught off base" with respect to his facts. There can be little doubt that much of his appeal, both to the academic world and to the general public, lay in his talent at*

[64] There are numerous stories told about his formidable memory. Much of the poetry which he had enjoyed during his youth, he could still recite. He told how on safari in Madagascar, he kept step as he walked to the rhythm of Scott's "The Lady of the Lake," which he could recite from beginning to end; at least so he said, but no one ever had the patience to hear him through. He once told a group of graduate students that he had taken Harold Lamb's book on Genghis Khan with him to Madagascar; since he had nothing else to read, he had read it several times and consequently knew it by heart. The book happened to be on his shelves so one of the students opened it at random reading a few lines. Linton then picked up the text and finished the page as the student checked him.

one and the same time commanding the facts authoritatively and stating them, with a novel twist of his own, in terms that all could understand.[65] ✤

Ralph Linton was not a "renaissance man" by any means, although he was exceedingly erudite. He had lived through the period in which any scholar could contribute to all of the subfields of anthropology. He kept himself abreast of physical anthropology and of Old and New World prehistory, and read widely in any science that interested him. There were, however, certain fields of interest in anthropology which he seemed to avoid. He was interested in comparative linguistics and in fact he was aware of the growing body of theory in structural linguistics. But Linton was not a linguist and he seemed to back away from linguistic analysis although it would have been helpful in developing his own thought. He also steered clear of kinships systems and kinship nomenclature. In a period in which practically all social and cultural anthropologists were indulging in a veritable orgy of kinship analysis, Linton does not once refer to a specific kinship system. He has excellent discussions of the nuclear family and its dependence upon larger kinship units, but he stops short of describing the varied forms these larger units take in different cultures. In one place, after describing the ascription of status through family, he dismisses kinship systems in the following way: "Describing and classifying relationship systems has been one of the favorite sports of anthropologists since the inception of the science, and the literature already available on the subject is voluminous. However, the differences between the systems are of little significance for our present discussion." [66] There are many anthropologists who would argue with him that the kinship system of a particular society may provide the key for some of the fundamental statuses and roles.

Perhaps the reason that he shied away from linguistics and from kinship system is that these fields require detailed formal analysis. They have something in common with mathematics, which he is said

[65] John Gillin, "Ralph Linton 1893–1953," in *American Anthropologist*, Vol. 56, No. 2, Part 1 (April 1954), p. 278.
[66] Ralph Linton, *The Cultural Backgrounds of Personality* (1945), p. 71.

not to have liked as a youth. It is doubtful that Ralph Linton would be at home with the present statistical trend in cultural anthropology. He would have felt happier with the new cognitive approach in social anthropology but even that he would have left to others. He was interested in broad concepts and theories rather than with the minutiae of analytical detail of cultures.

Linton began his professional career in anthropology when it was just emerging from antiquarianism and the museums to become a social science. Anthropologists were few in number and although scattered about the country they formed almost a club, at least, a "little society" in which everyone knew everyone else. Anthropologists had (and still have) a missionary fervor, a feeling that they should carry the new message to others and to convert. They were proud of their ability to live in and adapt to different cultures. Some of the sense that Ralph Linton had for his profession and for his relationship to his own society can be seen in some words which he wrote for *Twentieth Century Authors* just three days before his death:

❖ *Fortunately, as an ethnologist I have always been able to combine business with pleasure and have found my greatest satisfaction in friendships with men of many different races and cultures. I consider as my greatest accomplishments that I am an adopted member of the Comanche tribe, was accepted as a master carver by the Marquesas natives and executed commissions for them in their own art, am a member of the Native Church of North America (Peyote) according to the Quapaw rite, became a properly accredited ombiasy nkazo (medicine man) in Madagascar, and was even invited to join the Rotary Club of a middle western city.*[67] ❖

He also left anthropology richer in substance and theory with a solid role within the disciplines that make up the social sciences.

[67] Quoted in Gillin, 1954, p. 278.

PART II

Selections from the Writings of Ralph Linton

The main published works of Ralph Linton are the monographs and books which we have mentioned and cited frequently. His most important books are still in print, most of them in paperback editions. We have decided, therefore, to include here selections from his written work which are not so readily available to students and to the general public and which tell us something important about the man and his approach to anthropology.

Linton served two years with the Rainbow Division of the U. S. Army in France during the first World War. In spite of the hardships and horrors, he retained a romantic attitude toward the war. The short selection from his war poems entitled The Service, *and his essay* "Totemism and the A.E.F.," *which was first published in* American Anthropologist *(Vol. 26, No. 2, 1924), indicate that he also regarded the war as a sort of high-gear field expedition in anthropology.*

All selections have been reprinted with the permission of the publishers and of Mrs. Adelin Linton. Some of the selections have been slightly abridged.

The Service

✤ CAVALRY

Once we sat high enthroned o'er common men,
Tossed them a coin, or scornful, rode them down.
Fire leagues with them to rob us of our crown.
And now come wings to steal our eyes and speed.

Over long hills our dwindling columns wind,
Tired men and stumbling horses, on our trail
The tawny dust cloud in whose heart we see
Flutter of phantom pennons, glint of mail.

✤ ARTILLERY

Men built, our masters: now grown more than men,
We toil to serve them, sweat to make the flames
In their cold hearts, well knowing that our names
Will never lie upon those metal lips.

Our honor is the honor of our kings,
Breakers of Battle, Lords of Victory;
Great throats forever roaring to be fed
That slay, unwitting, foes we cannot see.

✤ INFANTRY

The fate of nations marches with our feet,
Their destinies weigh down our weary backs
When, with our shoulders stooping to our packs
We move in endless lines through sun and rain.

Ours the long slow horror of the trench
And ours at last, the glory when we meet
Foes face to face, and on our steel is laid
The final choice of victory or defeat.

✣ AVIATION

We are youth's heart made visible, who rise
On gleaming wings to greet the splendid sun,
Weary of earth's slow certainties, and run
Jousts with the elements to show our pride.

Last and most glorious chivalry, we meet
In single fight to win a single fame,
Sweep on victorious, or defeated pass
Like Archangels, trailing robes of flame.

Totemism and the A.E.F.

✣ Many modern anthropologists discount the supposed differences
in the mental processes of civilized and uncivilized peoples and hold
that the psychological factors which have controlled the growth of
the so-called primitive cultures are still at work in modern society.
It is difficult to obtain evidence on this point, and a record of the
development in the American army of a series of beliefs and practices
which show a considerable resemblance to the totemic complexes
existing among some primitive peoples may, therefore, be of interest.
The growth of one of these pseudo-totemic complexes can be fully
traced in the case of the 42nd or Rainbow Division. The name was
arbitrarily chosen by the higher officials and is said to have been
selected because the organization was made up of units from many
states whose regimental colors were of every hue in the rainbow.
Little importance was attached to the name while the division was
in America and it was rarely used by enlisted men. After the organization arrived in France, its use became increasingly common, and the
growth of a feeling of divisional solidarity finally resulted in its regular
employment as a personal appellation. Outsiders usually addressed
division members as "Rainbow," and to the question "What are
you?" nine out of ten enlisted men would reply "I'm a Rainbow."
This personal use of the name became general before any attitude
toward the actual rainbow was developed. A feeling of connection
between the organization and its namesake was first noted in Febru-

ary, 1918, five to six months after the assignment of the name. At this time it was first suggested and then believed that the appearance of a rainbow was a good omen for the division. Three months later it had become an article of faith in the organization that there was always a rainbow in the sky when the division went into action. A rainbow over the enemy's lines was considered especially auspicious, and after a victory men would often insist that they had seen one in this position even when the weather conditions or direction of advance made it impossible. This belief was held by most of the officers and enlisted men, and anyone who expressed doubts was considered a heretic and overwhelmed with arguments.

The personal use of the divisional name and the attitude toward the rainbow had both become thoroughly established before it began to be used as an emblem. In the author's regiment this phase first appeared in May, when the organization came in contact with the 77th Division which had its namesake, the Goddess of Liberty, painted on its carts and other divisional property. The idea was taken up at once, and many of the men decorated the carts and limbers in their charge with rainbows without waiting for official permission. As no two of the painted rainbows were alike, the effect was grotesque and the practice was soon forbidden. Nevertheless it continued, more or less surreptitiously, until after the armistice, when it was finally permitted with a standardized rainbow.

The use of rainbows as personal insignia appeared still later, in August or September. The history of the development of shoulder insignia in the American army is well known and need not be given here. The idea apparently originated with the Canadian forces, but the A.E.F. received it indirectly through one of the later American organizations which had adopted it before their arrival in France. The use of such insignia became general in the rear areas before it reached the divisions at the front. The first shoulder insignia seen by the author's regiment were worn by a salvage corps and by one of the newer divisions. This division was rumored to have been routed in its first battle, and it was believed that its members were forced to wear the insignia as punishment. The idea thus reached the 42nd Division under unfavorable auspices, but it was immediately taken up and passed through nearly the same phases as the use of painted insignia on divisional property. The wearing of shoulder insignia was at first forbidden by some of the regimental commanders, but even while it was proscribed many of the men carried insignia with them and pinned them on whenever they were out of reach of their officers. They were worn by practically all members of the division when in the rear areas, and their use by outsiders, or even by the men sent to the division as replacements, was resented and punished. In the case of replacements, the stricture was relaxed as they became recognized members of the group. . . .

By the end of the war, the A.E.F. had become organized into a series of well defined, and often mutually jealous, groups, each of which had its individual complex of ideas and observances. These complexes all conformed to the same general pattern but differed in content. The individual complexes bound the members of each group together and enabled them to present a united front against other groups. In the same way the uniformity of pattern gave a basis for mutual understanding and tolerance and united all the groups against persons or organizations outside the system.

The conditions in the American army after these group complexes had become fully developed may be summarized as follows:

(1) A division of the personnel into a number of groups conscious of their individuality;

(2) the possession by each of these groups of a distinctive name derived from some animal, object, or natural phenomenon;

(3) the use of this name as a personal appellation in conversation with outsiders;

(4) the use of representations of the group namesake for the decoration of group property and for personal adornment, with a taboo against its use by members of other groups;

(5) a reverential attitude toward the group namesake and its representations;

(6) in many cases, an unformulated belief that the group namesake was also a group guardian capable of giving omens.

Almost any investigator who found such a condition existing among an uncivilized people would class these associated beliefs and practices as a totemic complex. It shows a poverty of content when contrasted with the highly developed totemism of the Australians or Melanesians, but is fully as rich as the totemic complexes of some of the North American Indian tribes. The main points in which it differs from true totemism are the absence of marriage regulations, of beliefs in descent from, or of blood relationship with, the totem, and of special rites or observances to propitiate the totem. Each of these features is lacking in one or another of the primitive complexes which are usually classed as totemic and one of the most important, marriage regulation, is clearly a function of the clan or gentile system of organization and occurs in primitive groups for which totemism can not be proved.

It seems probable that both the A.E.F. complexes and primitive totemism are results of the same social and supernaturalistic tendencies. The differences in the working out of these tendencies can readily be accounted for by the differences in the framework to which they have attached themselves and in the cultural patterns which have shaped their expression. In the army, the military unit offered a crystallization point for these tendencies, and this precluded the development of marriage regulations or of a belief in the common [descent] of the group. The American culture pattern stimulated the development of the eponymous and decorative features, but offered formulae for the rationalization of the relation felt to exist between the group and its namesake, or for the development of observances for the namesake's propitiation. In primitive groups, on the other hand, the same tendencies usually crystallized about a clan or gentile system, and the marriage regulation features of this system became incorporated into the complex. Membership in the clan or gens was based on common descent, and in a group which drew no clear line between mankind and the rest of nature, the idea of blood relationship provided a convenient formula for the explanation of the group-namesake relation. Animistic or polytheistic concepts, and the existence of observances for the propitiation of a number of supernatural beings, afforded a pattern for the development of religious attitudes and special observances in connection with the namesake.

Even if we are willing to admit the essential unity of the tendencies

84

which produced the army complexes on one hand and the totemic complexes on the other, it does not follow that the observed development of the army complexes will throw much light on the history of primitive totemism. Even in the army no universal rule of evolution was evident, for although the starting-points were always the group and name, the other features appeared in different order in the various units. The ease and rapidity with which the army complexes were developed suggests that the tendencies underlying them were deep-seated and only awaited a chance for expression. The importance of diffusion in the growth of these complexes is suggestive, and the army conditions may afford a clue to the true significance of some totemic phenomena. The often-quoted example of the Australian who declared he was a kangaroo is a case in point. The author repeatedly heard soldiers declare that they were sunsets, wild cats, etc. and it would have required a good deal of questioning to obtain any coherent explanation of the relation which they felt existed between themselves and their namesakes. Such a cross-examination would have been impossible with the limited vocabulary of a trade jargon and very difficult with an ordinary interpreter. Although the army attitudes and practices were definite enough, their background was emotional rather than rational and the average soldier never attempted to formulate the ideas underlying them. Explanations elicited by questioning would be made up on the spur of the moment and would represent only his individual opinion. It seems probable that in primitive groups also a whole series of attitudes and practices could be developed without the individual feeling any need for their rationalization until he was confronted by some anthropological investigator.

During his expedition to Madagascar, Linton wrote several essays for the general public which were published in The Atlantic Monthly. "Witches of Andilamena" is one of these and it appeared in that magazine in 1927. We have reproduced it here not only for its literary merit but because it indicates his sensitivity and keenness as an observer.

Witches of Andílamena

✤ I doubt if I ever should have heard of the witches of Andíla-
mena if I had not taken the house on the hill. I wondered at the time
why it stood vacant, for it was one of the best in the village, and the
rental, three dollars and twenty-five cents a month, was ridiculously
low even for the back country of Madagascar. I should have been
warned by the owner's eagerness to rent it and by the fact that he
hardly bargained at all, but a careful examination showed nothing
wrong and it seemed ideal for my purpose. It stood on a slope, so
that there was very little mud, and was far enough from the village
to give some privacy. Moreover, a single night in the regular rest
house had shown that that was out of the question for a month's
stay. I still do not understand how its blood-thirsty inhabitants contrived to keep alive between the infrequent visits of white men.

Late afternoon saw me comfortably installed, and when the cook
reported that he had found a can of corned beef (United States
army stores, age eight years) in the Chinaman's store, I felt altogether at peace with the world. Wishing to take a look around, I
strolled up to the crest of the hill, about a hundred yards behind
the house. When I reached it I found that it had been leveled off
to form a small plateau, on which stood three large tombs. The slope
hid these from the house, but I felt sure that I had found the reason
for its standing vacant. The natives have a lively fear of ghosts. As
the tombs were evidently very old and seemed neglected, I ventured
to climb to the top of the highest and seat myself on its fallen
memorial stone.

The sun went down with tropical swiftness, the clouds began to
glow, the hills took on new and ever-changing colors. Forgetful of
everything else, I sat there until the stars came out and the last band
of light faded from the lake. As I rose to go I heard an exclamation
from somewhere down the slope and the sound of feet running.
Some native passing by must have seen my figure against the sky and
I laughed, knowing that he probably thought he had seen a ghost.

It had been a long, hard day and we all turned in early. My own bed was set up in the front room; Rabary, my interpreter, had a smaller room running across the right end of the house; and the cook slept in the kitchen. They closed every possible crack in their quarters, for they were civilized enough to have acquired a great fear of night air from the French. I left both my windows open, for I knew that with a people as wild as the Sihanaka there was little chance of theft. I was disturbed a good deal during the night by the hooting of owls. Once when I was asleep, a call came so loud and close that it awakened me with a jump. I thought one of the birds must have blundered into the room, and got up and lit a light to look for it, but found nothing.

At breakfast I noticed that both Rabary and the cook looked unhappy; both said that they had slept poorly. When I came back from my morning's work in the town there were no signs of dinner, only a small native boy with a message from the cook that he had had to go to see a relative and did not know when he would get back. This meant that he had left for good, forfeiting a week's pay I owed him. It was impossible to get another, and after one or two attempts I gave it up and took my meals with the missionary. When I told Rabary this he asked very earnestly whether the missionary would not have a bed for me as well. He was sure I should be much more comfortable there, and he would stay with a friend in the village. I said I was all right where I was, and thought no more about it.

The second night in the house was a repetition of the first, with the owls busy, and again I was awakened by a call which seemed to come from inside the room. I did not get up this time, and toward morning the calls quieted down and I fell into a heavy sleep.

It was bright daylight when I awoke and as I lay half dozing I noticed that some of the papers had fallen from my table to the floor. Then I saw something that brought me up standing. One of the sheets bore the unmistakable print of a rather small, muddy bare foot. I called to Rabary and told him a thief had been there during the night and asked him to help me check up and find what was missing.

He shook his head. "I think that there are not the things lost," he said. "The Sihanaka are a race very savage. There are not any thieves of here."

"Well, then," I asked, "what the deuce did someone crawl in through my window for?"

"I think it is one mpamosavy. I think he wants to make the charms against you or the other things of that sort. One tells me in the village yesterday this is a very bad place for all people after dark. One said the mpamosavy rode the last man here living like a saddle ox one night so that he was soon dead. I think it is much more better for us to discover a place of sleeping in the village, but if you wish not I will rest here with you. I am a good Christian of many years and I believe not that the mpamosavy spells can make harm to us. I am for three years in Europe and I know it is all foolishness. Also I am now a man old, without wife or child, and I have contrived all arrangements for the final disposal of my properties. I think is it better we go away during the night, but if you stay here I stay here."

I already knew a good deal about the mpamosavy, the Madagascar counterparts of European witches and warlocks, but I had hardly hoped to meet any of them, for they are usually very shy of interfering with white men. They have a reputation of being expert poisoners, but they never carry weapons on their night expeditions and are quite harmless to those who do not fear their spells. I really felt rather elated at having a chance for a little first-hand experience of them.

At dinner that night I mentioned my visitor to the missionary, and he agreed with Rabary that the invader was probably a mpamosavy. He had been the victim of their attentions himself when he first arrived and had found it hard to keep servants, but the importation of a mixed bulldog and mastiff the size of a well-grown calf had put a sudden stop to their activities. It seemed that the dog was immune to spells and he never accepted food from natives. The missionary had never seen a mpamosavy and said very few people had, even among the natives. It was said that they stripped completely before going out on their night runnings and painted and oiled themselves so that it was impossible to catch or recognize them. They danced upon the tombs, rode cattle, and played all sorts of queer and seemingly purposeless Halloween tricks, but they also sold and administered poisons and would guarantee to get rid of an enemy for you. Like European witches, they often had familiars in the shape of owls, cats, or snakes. In the parts of the island which were Christian they sometimes broke into the churches and performed travesties of the regular service, somewhat like the mediaeval Black Mass. In general they had little malice toward the Christians and a rather kindly feeling toward the vazaha (Europeans), for the latter had abolished the poison ordeals which took a heavy toll of them in the old days. Their real enemies were the ombiasy, or benevolent sorcerers, who knew how to cure their poisons and counteract their spells.

It was with something very much like pleasurable anticipation that I settled down to my work that evening. About nine o'clock there came a sharp knock at the door. I opened it, but there was no one there. A few minutes later the same thing happened again. Then Rabary came in from his room looking rather gray around the lips and said that the mpamosavy were trying to pull his shutter open. He had been wakened by its creaking and by the scratching of their nails as they tried to get a grip on it. I pointed out that if they really wanted to enter they could come in through either of my windows, for they were both wide open, but he did not relish the idea and I finally closed and bolted my shutters. A few moments later Rabary gripped my arm and pointed toward the door, and I saw that the latch was being slowly and noiselessly lifted from the outer side. Then something pressed against the door so hard that it creaked and bulged inward. This was too much, so I went outside and made a thorough search around the house and the kitchen, but I found nothing. When I got back Rabary said he had seen a death's head looking in at him through the half-open door. We waited about an hour; then, as there were no further manifestations, turned in and spent the rest of the night undisturbed.

I made a long trip the next day and got back so late that it was nearly ten o'clock before I settled down to list my specimens and write up my notes. I was working with my back toward one of the open windows, and in a pause of the typewriting I was sure that I heard a slight scraping noise on the sill behind me. I turned quickly and thought I caught a glimpse of something white or yellow disappearing at the side of my window, but could not be sure. A few minutes later I heard the gentle scratching again. I did not want to be "had" a second time, so I typed on for a little while, then stopped, stretched, and took off my shoes. These were of the trench variety, weighing about four pounds apiece, and I knew that they would make excellent missiles. I laid them to the right of my chair, where I could reach them with the minimum motion, and when I heard the scratching again I whirled and let drive with all my force. I distinctly saw something this time and I heard a grunt that made me hope I had scored a hit, but although I got to the window as quickly as I could there was nothing there. A search next day proved that the enemy had retired in good order, for he had taken the shoe with him.

Nothing happened the next night or the next, and I began to think the incident was closed. Rabary, on the other hand, got more and more nervous. He insisted that the witches would have changed from play to earnest after one of them was hit, and that they were quiet because they were preparing serious trouble and wanted to get us off our guard.

I began to believe him when, on the third morning, he pointed out that someone had smeared our threshold and lintel with oil during the night, for this is a sure sign of an attempt to lay a spell on someone who will pass through the doorway. However, I had more important things to think of, for fate threw a very valuable specimen into my hands.

Early one morning a man came to me apparently laboring under great fear or excitement, and begged me to come with him to see something he had at his house. When we arrived he carefully closed the door and window, and, going to a hiding place under the eaves, drew out a long parcel, which he handed to me and asked me to undo. I found that it contained a four-sided, rapier-like iron instrument nearly five feet long and a polished black cow horn filled with a mixture of little sticks, beads, and bits of silver. I recognized the horn instantly as an ody or charm, but the iron instrument was new to me. The owner insisted that I buy both at my own price and seemed to be in a pitiful state of terror, actually shaking all over. He explained that he had become a Christian some months ago, but before that he had been an ombiasy. He had derived his powers as such from the charm and iron stave which I then held, and when he became a Christian he had been at a loss what to do with them. As they had been able to help him before, they were now equally potent to harm him, and the only way for him to escape dire consequences was to find someone who would pay him for them so that they could be formally transferred. He had had a bad spill in the lake the day before, which had brought matters to a head.

I told him that I should be glad to relieve him of them if he would tell me exactly what were their virtues and how they should be used, and I found him more than willing to comply. The ody was of a common sort designed to bring good fortune, but the staff had rarer virtues. It could turn away bullets in battle or render void the most powerful spell, while the lightest touch from it would blast and kill a snake or a witch like a stroke of lightning. It seemed a handy thing to have around the house under the circumstances, and I carried it home concealed in a length of bamboo. Once there, I stood it up in the corner, in plain sight, hoping that some of my native visitors might be able to add new details about its powers.

There was an old native man who had half attached himself to my household, dropping in for a chat whenever he passed by and bringing small odds and ends to sell. He was especially captivated by my type-writer and would squat by the hour watching me work it, so I paid no attention to him when I was busy.

This afternoon he came in and was just settling down against the wall when the staff caught his eye. He gave a smothered ejaculation and stood up hastily, drawing his mantle across his mouth, then started for the door. When I rose he retreated to the far side of the room, trembling violently, and as I came toward him he fell flat and seized me by the ankles, a most unpleasant sensation. With his face on my shoes he began to talk rapidly. As my Malagasy was not equal to the occasion, I called in Rabary, who interrogated him for some time. What he said was briefly this:—

He admitted that he was a mpamosavy and begged me not to kill him. He would do anything I wished if I would put my staff away and promise not to hurt him. He would never have made spells against me if he had known that I had it. He and the other mpamo-savy would never have thought of interfering with a vazaha if one of their number had not seen me walking about on a tomb in the twilight. From this they had concluded that I must be a mpamosavy myself and that I wanted to buy charms. They thought I must have come to Madagascar to increase my powers, just as they themselves liked to get charms from other tribes. Everybody knew that such charms were stronger than one's own. The tombs on the little plateau behind my house were one of their favorite dancing places, and the owl calls I had heard on the first and second nights of my stay were meant to let me know that they were about and to invite me to come out and join them. On both nights one of them had come into my room through the window and given a call beside my bed, to make quite sure I heard. By the third night they had concluded that I could not be a mpamosavy after all and had tried to frighten me in a spirit of mischief rather than spite. My indifference had annoyed them and after the affair of the shoe they turned spiteful. They did not like to have anyone living so near the scene of their night revels, and as their tricks had failed to drive me away they had begun to make spells against my health and business.

My captive's work had been to smuggle malevolent charms into my house, and I do not doubt that during much of the time he was squatting near me, ostensibly watching me at work, he had really been repeating spells against me. When I threatened him with the staff he began to unearth charms from various hiding places in the room. One, some herbs tied up in a scrap of red cloth, had been put behind some maps in a corner. Another, which seemed to be mostly a mixture of castor oil and honey, had been smeared under the edge of my table. The most curious had been thrust under a loose board beside the door. It was a knot formed by two intertwined tendrils. Such knots are commonly used as love charms, but can also be made to breed discord if prepared with the proper spells. This one was designed to cause quarrels between myself and my interpreter.

When he insisted that all the charms had been removed I began to question him about the general activities of the mpamosavy and

92

he talked quite freely, even giving some information about the manufacture and use of poisons. When I tried to get at the beliefs underlying their black magic, however, I found myself against a blank
wall. The only explanation he would or could give was that all
mpamosavy did certain things and would not be mpamosavy if they
did not. Even the custom of dancing on tombs was explained by the
same formula.

I gave it up at last, as it was growing late, and turned to arrangements for the future. It was plain that the man would prove a mine
of information and I dealt gently with him, promising not to hurt
him or tell his neighbors that he was a wizard. In return he promised
to give me a good collection of witch charms, to see that the witches
left me alone in future, and to return my shoe. To ensure the carrying
out of his part of the contract I took a lock of his hair and the dust
from the floor under his right foot. As magicians we both knew that
with these I could work his destruction, body and soul, if he played
me false. At parting I gave him a little money to soothe his wounded
pride, and he seemed quite cheerful and even ventured to boast a
little of his powers. He promised to return in three days, that length
of time being required for the making of certain charms he would
bring.

The next morning I found the shoe outside my door, but by noon
I was down with one of those short but violent attacks of fever that
make Madagascar so dangerous to white men. I have only a hazy
recollection of what happened during the next three or four days, but
I seem to remember a visit from several natives and that they stood
outside the door and talked for some time. When the fever had
broken, Rabary told me that the people in the village had been very
much afraid that I should die and that the government would punish
them if I did. When I was able to work again I sent for the wizard,
and when he did not come I went to his house. The door was un-
fastened, but there was no one there and the ashes of his cooking fire
were quite cold. None of his neighbors could tell me anything about
him. At last I called on the headman of the village and asked him if
he knew where the man was.

"Nobody knows," he said. "He has gone away."

"It is strange," I said, "that he did not take his clothes with him."
"Yes, it is strange," he agreed, "but perhaps he does not need them."

The two papers, "Crops, Soils, and Culture" and "The Change from Dry Rice to Wet Rice Cultivation," both appeared after the publication of Linton's important book The Study of Man, *but they are examples of his profound and continuing interest in cultural ecology—of man's dependence upon the land, the crops, the technology, and the social structure. The first of these two articles was published in* The Maya and Their Neighbors *(Appleton-Century, 1940), a volume dedicated to Alfred Tozzer by his former students and colleagues. The second is an excerpt from Linton's contribution on the Tanala in* The Individual and His Society *by Abram Kardiner (Columbia University Press, 1939).*

Crops, Soils, and Culture in America

✤ Anthropologists have long recognized the effect of environment on culture but the interrelations are so complex that it is almost impossible to grasp them in their entirety. The potentialities of any environment for any society are a function of the interaction of the natural environment and the society's techniques for exploiting it. Thus the potential food supply in any region will be determined, for an agricultural people, not only by climate and soil but also by the nature of the crops which they possess and their methods of raising them. To cite a single example, the introduction of wheat and of European methods of cultivation have opened to agricultural settlements thousands of square miles in North America which were not available to Indian groups raising maize by aboriginal methods. It is the purpose of this paper to point out certain of these interrelations which seem to have been overlooked and to suggest their possible influence on the growth of American cultures and on the establishment of particular patterns of settlement in various regions.

It is generally recognized that complex technology and elaborate political organization can only develop or survive in the presence of fairly dense populations. It is also recognized that the possible density of population in any region is normally linked with the local food supply. The exceptions to this rule which occur as a result of modern methods of transport and communication can be ignored in the present discussion. However, it is less generally recognized that the significance of a food supply for population support depends not only on its quantity but also on its qualities. The number of persons who can be fed from a certain area is determined by considerations of a balanced ration and will be only slightly affected by a surplus of any one of the elements necessary for such a ration.

What constitutes a balanced ration is, in itself, an exceedingly complex problem. In spite of the rapid progress of research along this line we are still very much in the dark as to the minimum amount of vitamins and minerals necessary to insure health and it is quite possible that certain as yet unsuspected substances may enter into the picture. The writer is not an expert on nutrition and the present discussion will, therefore, be confined to one of the simplest aspects of the problem, that of a protein and starch balance. There seems to be abundant evidence that although our species can adapt itself to a starchless diet, it cannot survive on one which lacks a certain minimum of proteins and fats. Thus there are human groups who live exclusively on meat and/or fish or on a combination of meat and dairy products, but there are no human groups who live on starch foods without the addition of proteins. This means that an agriculture which confines itself to the raising of starch crops cannot form the exclusive basis of a people's food economy.

If we turn to the Old World we find that throughout most of Eurasia and Africa a balanced ration was provided by a combination of starch crops and dairy products. It was the latter rather than the simple domestication of animals which, in combination with agriculture, made possible large and settled populations. Milking the herd provided many times the proteins and fats which might have been obtained by killing from the herd. In further Asia, where the dairying pattern never penetrated, the need for protein was met in some regions by a local protein crop, the soya bean, and in others by the rearing of pigs and chickens, supplemented by fishing and local small game. Where the people were within reach of the sea sufficient proteins and fats could be obtained by fishing alone. This was the situation which obtained in most of Oceania, where the local crops were almost exclusively starch crops. In Polynesia, where there was no native game, a tribe which was cut off from the sea was in desperate straits even when it had abundant land for agriculture. In Melanesia, where there is some game in the larger islands, we find that interior populations are usually much sparser than the quantity of land available for agriculture would seem to justify and that there is frequently a trade in fish between the coastal and interior tribes.

In America there were comparatively few domestic animals and those present made only a slight contribution to the aboriginal food supply. Dogs and turkeys were eaten in some places but were luxuries rather than staples, while the South American llama and related species were never milked and were too valuable for wool and transport to be killed except on ceremonial occasions. Proteins and fats had to be obtained by hunting and fishing, by gathering wild plants, or by raising special crops. Actually, all the higher American cultures were based on a combination of starch and protein crops just as all the civilizations of the Old World were based on a combination of starch crops and domestic animals.

In his exceedingly stimulating article, "American Agricultural Origins"[1] Dr. Carl Sauer has stressed the large number of starch crops raised by the American Indians. He concludes on the basis of several sorts of evidence that most of these crops were domesticated independently and in different regions and suggests the probability of the independent invention of agriculture at several points in South and Middle America. He further concludes that these original centers of agriculture were all located in valleys or plateaus of moderate altitude, that is, in inland regions.[2] This point is of considerable im-

---

[1] CARL SAUER, "American Agricultural Origins;" in Essays in Anthropology in Honor of Alfred Kroeker, edited by Robert L. Lowie, Berkeley, 1936.
[2] *Ibid.*, pp. 283–84.

portance to the present discussion, for it means that the earliest American farmers were cut off from sea fishing, one of the surest and most abundant sources of proteins and fats.

In contrast with the multiplicity of American starch crops the number of protein crops was decidedly limited. There were only two of any importance, the peanut and the bean, the latter in numerous varieties. Recent investigations of Russian botanists, summarized by Dr. Sauer,[3] indicate that the peanut was originally a native of Brazil, the bean of Middle America. Whether the domestication of these two plants was contemporaneous with the domestication of starch crops in the same localities cannot be determined at present. However, maize appears in our own Southwest in much older cultural horizons than does the bean, and if the two crops appeared in Middle America at the same time it is hard to see why one should have been diffused northward without the other. It seems probable, therefore, that maize culture was established in Middle America before bean culture.

An inland people who had no domestic food animals and who raised only starch crops would have great difficulty in developing or maintaining a dense population. They would have to depend upon hunting and wild foods such as nuts or legumes for their proteins and fats. This would set a fairly low upper limit to the size of population and especially of localized aggregates. To hunt and gather wild foods successfully the people would have to live in small and widely spaced communities. In time such farmer-food gatherers might develop considerable skill in cultivation, but a mere increase in the quantity of starch foods raised would not solve their problem. There would be a definite ceiling, set by the supply of wild proteins, beyond which their population could not increase without encountering dietary deficiencies. This, in turn, would set a limit to the level of culture which they could maintain. Large aggregates can afford to support specialists while small aggregates cannot.

Let us assume for the sake of argument that agriculture was invented, and various starch crops domesticated, independently in

[3] *Ibid.*, pp. 289–90.

several places in the New World. If so, there must have been many communities scattered over the two continents who had the habit of crop raising but who were subject to the limitations on population growth imposed by protein deficiency. The domestication of a local protein-yielding plant, or the introduction of such a plant through diffusion, would remove this limitation. A new and much higher ceiling for population would be set, depending mainly upon the amount of arable land available, and until this ceiling was reached there would be boom times. The size of local aggregates could be greatly increased and the stage set for rapid cultural advance. If the protein crop was a diffused one, this change might occur with great speed. To a people already familiar with agriculture the acceptance of a new crop is an easy matter, as we know from the rapidity with which American food plants spread through the Old World after the discovery of America.

It is interesting to check this hypothesis against the known development of culture in the Southwest. Here we have indisputable evidence of a comparatively brief period of very rapid cultural advance with a strong suggestion that this was correlated with a great increase in population. The period of advance seems to have been preceded by a much longer period, lower limits still unknown, during which the development of culture was slow while it was followed by another long period of comparative culture stabilization. It also seems that the period of rapid advance cannot be accounted for on the basis of sudden contact with and borrowing from some other culture. The Anasazi line of culture development runs uninterruptedly from the Basket Makers to the builders of the great pueblos, and unbroken evolutionary series can be traced for most of the elements present. We must conclude that Basket Maker culture received a sudden stimulus of some sort. We know that, although the Basket Makers raised corn and squashes from early times, the bean does not appear in the Southwest until shortly before the period of culture flowering. It seems probable, therefore, that the introduction of this protein crop, with the consequent raising of the population ceiling, was responsible for the sudden release of cultural energy.

There are suggestions for such a period of rapid change and advance in the Southeast also, although the evidence there is much less con-

98

clusive and an exact chronology is lacking. The finding of seeds of domesticated and improved rag weed and amaranth in Bluff Dwellers sites and the fact that these crops seem to have been allowed to lapse by the period of first European contact may indicate an independent development of agriculture in this region. Such evidence as we have for the introduction of corn and beans into the Southeast seems to indicate that, if they were not introduced together, the time interval separating the two introductions was short. The sudden advance of Southeastern culture may, therefore, have been due to the introduction of a maize-bean complex into a region where agricultural techniques were already known but where the crops were inadequate. Such an introduction would provide a balanced ration at a single stroke and make possible a rapid population increase.

Even in Middle America there seems to be evidence of a period of rapid cultural advance. Although the Maya civilization did not rise out of darkness as abruptly as once supposed, its sudden flowering in the Old Empire certainly suggests some stimulating factor. May this not have been the addition of beans to a pre-existing agricultural complex? The apparent priority of maize over bean culture in Middle America has already been noted.

Other things being equal, one might expect the period of rapid population advance and cultural flowering to continue in any region until all available new land had been brought under cultivation. After this the population would decline with the diminishing food supply until it stabilized at a level which could be maintained by reutilization of land. This level would be determined by a combination of the nature of the local soils and of the techniques for exploiting them provided by the particular culture. The latter would, of course, include not only methods of tillage and fertilization or crop rotation but also facilities for land clearance. The importance of weed growth to land reutilization has been brought out by recent researches of the Carnegie Foundation in Yucatan.[4]

American agriculture, outside two or three centers of high civilization, was comparatively crude. There was only sporadic use of fertilizers or crop rotation, the main method for restoring used soils being

[4] R. A. EMERSON, A Preliminary Survey of the Milpa System of Maize Culture..., Cornell University, Ithaca, mimeograph.

simple fallowing. Soils naturally varied with the locality, but there were certain climatic factors which were of importance to both soil exhaustion and rejuvenation. Where rains are light, the substances necessary to crop growth remain in the upper levels of the soil where they are readily available. The fertility of most desert lands when water can be brought to them is proverbial. In tropical regions of heavy rainfall, on the other hand, the warm rains leach out the mineral content of the surface soil and carry it down beyond the reach of ordinary crop roots. In moist temperate regions the conditions are intermediate, depending on quantity and season of precipitation. Thus a soil of given mineral content will grow crops longest under semi-arid conditions, for a shorter time under moist temperate ones, and for a still shorter time in a tropical rain belt.

Closely connected with these differences in moisture and temperature is the factor of weed growth. This is of the utmost importance to agriculturalists who lack metal tools. In semi-arid regions weed growth is slow and comparatively scanty, making the annual reconditioning of cleared fields easy. In moist temperate ones the growth is more rapid and abundant, but it reaches its climax in regions of tropical rainfall where the growth is so rapid and dense that almost as much labor is required to reclear a field used even the previous year as to clear long-standing jungle.

These factors of soil fertility and weed growth united to impose different patterns of soil utilization in different climatic areas. While the Southwestern tribes could grow corn on the same lands generation after generation, the Indians of the Eastern Woodlands had to change their cultivation every three or four years due to a combination of soil exhaustion and weed seed accumulation. In the wet tropics the same factors, in increased intensity, made it difficult to crop a field more than two years in succession and desirable to clear new fields every year. Recuperation of the land through fallowing followed a similar order. Desert soils recuperated very slowly and areas which had been depleted by long cultivation had to be abandoned for many years. In temperate regions the recuperation was more rapid, due to the heavier plant growth, while in jungle areas fifteen to twenty years were required for complete recovery.

Both the total population of an area and the possible size of residential aggregates are intimately related to these factors of soil exhaustion, weed growth, and soil recuperation. With Indian techniques of agriculture the long-term stabilization point for the population of any area was determined by the possibilities of turnover in fallow and cultivated land. A tribe might actually have bred up to the limits of its assured long-term agricultural food supply while much of its territory appeared to be unused. The possible size of the village groups within the tribe was set by the amount of food which could be raised on land exploitable from the village. The extent of this zone of exploitation was roughly determined by the distance to which a man could travel, work in the fields, and return on the same day. When it was necessary to guard the fields against raiders, the zone was correspondingly narrowed.

Given the rich soils of semi-arid regions, the scanty weed growth and crops suited to local conditions, large settlements could be established and remain on the same site for several generations. Under such circumstances the population would become so thoroughly rooted that, when soil exhaustion did make itself felt, the people would tend to cling to their settlement until the last possible moment. Perhaps the long dwindling of population which is evident for some of the Southwestern ruined pueblos may have been due to progressive soil exhaustion as well as to the drought period. With the slowness of soil recuperation, fields that had once been exhausted could not be reutilized for so long a time that the same group would rarely return to them at all.

In tropical rain forests, on the other hand, the soil exhaustion and weed growth were so rapid that villages as large as those of the Southwest would have had to move every two or three years. Actually, the pattern in the American rain forest areas seems to have been that of much smaller local aggregates, but even so a village rarely remained in the same place for as much as a generation. The tribes here had the habit of movement and seem to have drifted long distances with ease. In moist temperate regions, such as the eastern United States, village movement was also necessary as long as the zone of exploitation was limited by the common residence of the community's members. However, the villagers could remain in one place for a generation or more and moved with corresponding reluctance. Moreover, the rather rapid recuperation of the land under fallowing made it possible for a village to move about within a fairly restricted area, returning to the same territory time after time. This seems to have been the condition which existed among the proto-historic Iroquois and some of the northern agricultural Siouan tribes such as the Winnebago. However, it was most characteristic of the tribes living on the northern margins of the eastern agricultural area, regions in which fortified villages were useful for defense against the neighboring hunting groups. It is interesting to note that whenever this threat was removed, as in the time of Iroquois League dominance, the village populations tended to spread out and the community to remain in the same place for longer intervals.

This fact may provide a clue to the origin of the type of community organization found in the Southeast and in many parts of Middle America. In both these regions we find a development of confederacies or other large political groupings which made large areas comparatively safe from attack. Soils were rich enough here to permit villages to remain in one place long enough to take root. When the soil in the immediate neighborhood of the village began to be exhausted, safety from attack made it possible for the village to expand its zone of exploitation by having its members live at the more distant farms during the agricultural season. In due course of time it might come to be surrounded by isolated families or even hamlets whose inhabitants felt themselves members of the central community although they did not regularly reside there. Since the soil recuperated readily under fallowing, such an extended community might become very large without exceeding the assured year by year food supply. The community would be as firmly rooted in one place as a Southwestern pueblo, but would have quite different characteristics. In particular, the central town from which the scattered population had been derived would tend to become a community center, a place to which the whole group resorted for exchange of goods, councils, and ceremonies. This is the pattern which obtains for certain Guatemalan Indian towns today and which probably obtained for most of the Middle American cities of pre-European times. The great temples and squares for assembly found in these cities seem to be quite out of proportion to the apparent size of their constant populations but were adapted to the function of the cities as community centers. Very similar arrangements in town planning are found in our own Southeast where we know that a similar scattering of families on isolated farms existed. These resemblances between the Southeast and Middle America are probably due to a northward diffusion of the pattern, but their acceptance in the Southeast was justified by the similarity of community organization.

In the Southwest this type of community organization never developed. This may have been due in part to the lack of political organizations larger than single villages, with the consequent danger of attack on isolated families. However, soil may also have played a part. With the slowly exhausted, slowly rejuvenated soils of this region there was less stimulus to expanding a village's zone of exploitation while the area required for a really permanent settlement with alternate cultivation and fallowing would have been enormous. The Southwestern village was a highly localized, closely knit community which needed no focal point. Perhaps the failure of the Middle American community center type of town planning to diffuse into the Southwest is due to the fact that the needs to which it was a response did not exist here.

All cultural processes involve a multiplicity of causal factors which, in combination, produce a multiplicity of results. The writer would be the first to admit that the hypotheses which have just been advanced to account for certain observed phenomena of American cultures are much too simple. However, food is the most basic of human needs and the crops and soils from which the American Indians derived it deserve more attention than they have received to date.

The Change from Dry to Wet Rice Cultivation in Madagascar

✤ The culture we have described is that of the Tanala of the dry rice cultivation. Wet rice cultivation, which introduced so many elements in social change that the whole culture was eventually altered, was borrowed from their Betsileo neighbors to the east. It was at first an adjunct to dry rice carried on by individual families. Before the new method was introduced on a large scale, there were already rice swamps of permanent tenure, which never reverted to the village for reassignment. But land favorable for this use was very limited, because of natural factors. Thus there gradually emerged a group of land-owners, and with the process came a breakdown in the joint family organization. The cohesiveness of this older unit was maintained by economic interdependence and the need for cooperation. But an irrigated rice field could be tended by a single family, and its head need not recognize any claim to share it with anyone who had not contributed to its produce.

This group of permanent rice sites formed the nucleus of a perma-nent village, because the land could not be exhausted as was the land exploited by the dry method. As land suitable for wet rice near the village was presently all taken up, the landless households had to move farther and farther away into the jungle. So far away would they be that they could not return the same day. These distant fields also became household rather than joint family affairs.

The moving of the older unit from one land site to another had kept the joint family intact. But now single landless households were forced to move, while there were in the same unit landowners who had a capital investment and no incentive to move. The migrant groups were thus cross-sections of the original lineages. Each original village had a group of descendant villages, each one surrounded by irrigated fields and private ownership.

The mobile villages had been self-contained and endogamous. The settled villages were much less so. The joint family retained its reli-gious importance, based on the worship of a common ancestor, even after its component households had been scattered. Family members would be called together on ceremonial occasions, and thus the old village isolation broke down. Intermarriages became common. In this way, the transformation from independent villages to a tribal organi-zation took place.

The process brought further changes in the patterns of native war-fare. The old village had to be defended; but not at so great a cost nor with the necessity for permanent upkeep. When the village became permanent the defenses had to be of a powerful kind, involving big investments and permanent upkeep.

Slaves, who were of no economic significance in the old system, now acquired economic importance. This gave rise to new techniques of ransom. Thus the tribal organization grew in solidity, and with the change the old tribal democracy disappeared. The next step was a king at the head who exercised control over the settled elements but not over the mobile ones. The kingdom came to an end before any adequate machinery of government could be established. This king built himself an individual tomb, thus breaking an ancient custom.

The changes were, therefore, a king at the head, settled subjects, rudimentary social classes based on economic differences, and lineages of nothing but ceremonial importance. Most of the changes had already taken place among the Betsileo. The cooperative system made individual wealth impossible. Nor was the change devoid of serious stresses on the individual; a new class of interests, new life goals, and new conflicts came into being.

One of the Tanala clans, the Zafimaniry, was one of the first to take up the new wet rice cultivation. They continued it for a time, but finally abandoned it, and returned to the dry rice method. They offered as the reason for returning to the old method the fact that they had been attacked by an enemy, which scattered the men of the various households. The tribe tabooed the raising of wet rice, and still continues to refuse to take up wet rice despite depletion of the jungle.

Although we are not in possession of all the facts, and a great many unknown factors may have operated, we are justified in looking into the culture of the Betsileo for a contrast with the ultimate changes coincident with wet rice culture. The traditions of the Betsileo have it that there was a time when all people were equal and all land was held in common. Moreover, the cultural similarity to the Tanala leaves no doubt that in the main we are dealing with two cultures spring from a cognate source. Or to be more accurate, the changes we find in Betsileo culture were engrafted on a culture similar in all respects to the one we found in Tanala.

Whatever adventitious changes took place, basically we can regard Betsileo as the Tanala culture, after all the changes consequent upon wet rice has become consolidated, organized, and institutionalized. We are therefore observing an important experiment in the dynamics of social change.

In Betsileo society the gens is still the foundation of social life, descent being traced through the male line from a single ancestor. But the organization of the village as in Tanala culture is gone; it apparently disappeared according to the steps outlined above.

The local clan groups were administered by heads appointed by the king, one head for each gens. Members of several gentes live in the same village. Instead of free access to gens lands, as in Tanala culture, we have here a rigid system of ground rent levied on the land in the form of a proportion of rice produce.

Instead of the previous democracy as among the Tanala there is a rigid caste system with a king at the head, nobles, commoners, and slaves. The powers of the king are absolute over the life and property of everyone. The commoners are the bulk of the population, the nobles, to all intents, feudal lords whose chief control is over land by royal assignment; the slaves are war captives or their descendants.

The powers of the king far exceeded those of a lineage head in Tanala society and in some ways were greater than those of the ancestral ghosts. He could take the life, property, or wife of anyone; he could elevate and degrade the status of anyone at will, and no redress was possible. In accordance with these powers, a great many secondary mores which accentuate the enhanced prestige of the king are present. There are taboos about his person and concerning his children; there are special clothes forbidden to anyone else; special words must be used to designate the condition or anatomy of the king. A king was not sick, he was "cold." He did not have eyes, he has "clearness." The souls of dead kings were called Zanahary-so-and-so. Succession was decided from among the king's sons, but not necessarily the oldest. Notwithstanding his great powers and prestige, he might work like a commoner in the rice fields. Though his powers were absolute and he could not be dethroned, he could be counseled to mend his ways.

Though the king owned all the land, he allotted it for use on a basis which was a charter of ownership, revokable at his will. The king dispensed this land in quantities proportional to the importance of, and the potential return from, the individual concerned. He would give the biggest allotments in return for the greatest support. The large landowner, a noble, could now rent any portion of his land to tenant farmers, who would pay rent in the form of a proportion of produce. Land thus owned could be sold or bequeathed as long as it did not become subject to another king. In short, here was a feudal system of a kind.

The staple crop was rice by the wet method; but other crops were cultivated as well—manioc, maize, millet, beans, and sweet potatoes. The chief adjunct to wet rice cultivation was the possibility of transporting water by irrigation, a factor which added to the permanency of the whole organization and took something of the premium away from the swamps and valleys. Irrigation methods made it possible to use the terraced hillsides for agriculture. But control of irrigation, and even perhaps its installation, made a strong central power essential.

The significance of cattle was the same as in Tanala culture; they had little economic but high prestige value. Cows were used chiefly for sacrifice and hence an instrument of power with the gods. The chief source of meat food were chickens, as with the Tanala.

Parallel to the powers of the king were the powers of the father in the individual household; in Betsileo he exercised an unchecked absolutism. All property belonged to the father during the latter's lifetime except his wives' clothes and the gifts he might make to his wives or children. The profits from exploitation of the land went to him. The inheritance laws resembled those of the Tanala except that land could now be inherited.

In the life cycle of the individual we begin to note important changes. The approaching birth of a child is not announced, for fear of sorcery. The afterbirth is buried and various superstitions are connected with it. As in Tanala culture, some days are propitious for birth, others are not. A child born on a certain day (the equivalent of Sunday) must be thrown on the village rubbish heap for a while, or washed in a jug of dirty dishwater. This is supposed to avert evil destiny. The belief is that a child born on one of these unlucky days will destroy its family. Children born in the month of *Alakaosy* are killed either by drowning, or by having cattle walk over them. Should they survive these exposures, they are kept, with the due precaution of changing their destiny through an *ombiasy*. Adoption is frequent; so also is changing of names.

The basic disciplines are like those of the Tanala. But here in Betsileo society strong emphasis falls on the training in various shades of deference to elders and rank. Manners elevate the status of one individual as against another: the father is served separately, etc.

Incest taboos are the same as those of the Tanala, and observance is with the same general laxity. Premarital chastity is expected of women and punishment is sterility—as with the Tanala. The endogamy of marriage is now within caste lines, though elevation in status of a slave can take place. There is considerably more homosexuality than in Tanala.

The levirate is practiced in Tanala culture but not in Betsileo. A man who married his brother's widow would be strongly suspected of having killed his brother with sorcery or poison. Polygamy is the rule, as in Tanala.

The disciplinarian in Betsileo society is the father. He has the sole right to punish his children, a right which is, however, rarely exercised. Children may desert their parents in Betsileo, something which is almost inconceivable in Tanala. In one family eight children deserted their parents, whereupon the father changed his name to mean, "I have wiped away excrement for nothing."

The religion of Betsileo is much like that of Tanala; but significant changes can be noted. The rigid belief in fate is changed somewhat to mean that god arranges everything in advance. Sorcery (*mpamosavy*) is now the cause of illness, but the sorcerer is only an executive of god. We find new concepts in Betsileo culture which are unknown in Tanala. For example, god is angry if anyone oppresses the poor. There is a strong belief now in retaliation for aggression against anyone. A man is rich because his Zanahary is good.

The immediate supernatural executives are ghosts and spirits of various kinds. There are for example the *vazimba*, who once lived in the land of the Betsileo and were driven out. Their souls did not go to heaven but remained in the tombs and are, therefore, hostile. *Mpamosavy* bury bait in the tombs of the *vazimba* to kill the person from whom the bait was taken. They also believe in several other varieties of evil spirits in the form of birds or animals. The Betsileo make a clear distinction between life and soul. Life ceases with death, the soul continues. The soul may leave the body by breaking a taboo, through excessive chagrin or fright. The souls of the dead observe the same caste distinctions as obtained in life. The souls of the disowned are evil, and can seduce good souls to do mischief to their own families. A good funeral for a relative insures his good will after death. The soul of a king is transformed into a snake.

Possession by spirits is much more common than in Tanala. In the latter we noted occasional *tromba* (possession by a ghost), and very rarely *mpamosavy*. In Betsileo one is possessed by evil spirits. The incidence is very common and the manifestations much more severe. These spirit illnesses are due to either human or nonhuman spirits. In one type of possession (*aretondolo*) the victim sees these spirits which are invisible to everyone else. They persecute the victim in a large number of ways. They pursue him and he flees across the country; he may be dragged along and made to perform all varieties of stunts. But the remarkable thing is that the victim never shows marks of injury. These seizures come suddenly, and after the first attack, the victim is liable to others. His seizure ends in a spell of unconsciousness, from which he awakes normal. Another form of possession is called *salomanga*, which is possession by a once human spirit.

The chief method of worship is by means of sacrifice and thanks. The Betsileo make sacrifices for favors desired or received; they sacrifice for plenty and for scarcity. These is, however, a novelty in the form of taking a vow which in essence is a promise to make a sacrifice, usually a cow or fowl pending the outcome of certain events in the individual's favor. The rituals are filled with all kinds of repetitious ceremonials; the same thing must be done a certain number of times to be effectual.

The *ombiasy* has the same functions as in Tanala. He cures the sick, performs *sikidy*, designates good and bad days for undertakings, and makes charms. The *ombiasies* are as in Tanala, *nkazo* and *ndolo*, the latter being chiefly women.

There are in addition to the legitimate *ombiasies* the malevolent sorcerers, *mpamosavy*. These are very scarce in Tanala, but very numerous—or at least suspected to be so—in Betsileo. The practice is secret, and hereditary. The *mpamosavy* is an agent of Zanahary and is possessed by the god. These sorcerers do evil deeds at night, and run out of their homes naked except for a turban. Everyone is suspected of being *mpamosavy*. They work chiefly by planting charms in places where they can do harm. The techniques by which the *mpamosavy* work are similar to those in Tanala. One such charm is a small wooden coffin containing medicines and a small dead animal. When this is destroyed the charm is broken. Nail parings, hair cuttings, leftover food, clothing, earth from a footprint, can be used to injure its owner; urine, feces, and spittle are not so used. In Tanala we noted that these could not be used for malevolent magic as "bait." As a result in Betsileo all nail parings, hair cuttings, etc., are kept in one common heap. The charms used by *mpamosavy*, powerful in themselves, are strengthened and reinforced by evil ghosts. Anyone apprehended in the practice of *mpamosavy* is ostracized or driven into exile.

There is perhaps one additional concept in Betsileo culture not found in Tanala: the breaking of a taboo can be atoned for by an act of purification.

Much more general apprehension exists in Betsileo than Tanala, as shown by the increase in belief in omens, dreams, and superstitions. The difference is quantitative. Some of the superstitions are rather telling. When a person dies at the moment of a good harvest, he has been killed by his wealth. The superstitions all indicate some fear of retaliatory misfortune. The type of reasoning is largely by analogy. Thus, if anyone strikes a snake but does not kill it, the offender will suffer as the snake suffers; if it is sick he will be sick, if it dies, he will die.

There is also considerable increase in crime, stealing in particular, but also murder. For this latter crime there is indemnity and retaliation by vendetta. The Tanala do not engage in boxing; the Betsileo do. Suicide is very uncommon; but I have heard of a case of suicide in which the man vowed to use his soul to persecute the man who drove him to it. Blood brotherhood exists as in Tanala.

One additional custom should be noted, as of contrast to Tanala. There the village tomb contains all the dead. In Betsileo, burial was in individual family tombs, the women being laid on one side, the men on the other. The king's body was mummified, with special rituals insuring the liberation from the body of a small embryo which later turns into a snake. Tombs became one of the favorite ways of displaying wealth and ostentation. Technological development of weaving and pottery in Betsileo was very much more highly developed than in Tanala. However, the Betsileo made contact with several neighboring peoples where these arts were highly developed, whereas the Tanala did not.

In conclusion we can say that Tanala and Betsileo cultures were identical in the main. The differences are traceable to the change in productive methods from dry to wet rice cultivation. This is proven by several circumstances: The traditions in Betsileo indicate an old culture very like Tanala; the institutions of both indicate a common source, and many of them are still identical; the changes in Tanala were gradual, and were well on the way to becoming identical with Betsileo when the French took over; and finally some of the Tanala tribes took over the wet rice method and abandoned it because of the serious incompatibilities it created in the social structure. The spread of wet rice cultivation cannot be attributed solely to diffusion; wet rice culture was endemic in Tanala and coincident with dry rice. Its spread was favored largely by the exhaustion of the dry method. Hence in examining the changes secondary to this main innovation, we need not depend exclusively on diffusion for an explanation.

"Nativistic Movements," which was written for the centennial meeting of the American Ethnological Society, appeared in American Anthropologist (Vol. 45, No. 2, 1943).

Nativistic Movements

✣ At the time that the centennial meeting of the American Ethnological Society was planned, the writer was invited to contribute a paper on nativistic movements in North America. When he attempted to prepare this it soon became evident that there was a need for a systematic analysis of nativistic phenomena in general. Although the Social Science Research Council's Committee on Acculturation had made some progress in this direction much remained to be done. The present paper is an attempt to to provide such a systematic analysis and is presented in the hope that its formulations may be modified and expanded by further research.

The first difficulty encountered in the study of nativistic movements was that of delimiting the field. The term "nativistic" has been loosely applied to a rather wide range of phenomena, resembling in this respect many other terms employed by the social sciences. For the writer to determine arbitrarily which of several established usages is to be considered correct and which incorrect is not only presumptuous but also one of the surest ways to promote misunderstanding of the theoretical contributions he hopes to make. The only satisfactory definition under such circumstances is one based upon the common denominators of the meanings which have come to be attached to the term through usage. With this as a guide, we may define a nativistic movement as, "Any conscious, organized attempt on the part of a society's members to revive or perpetuate selected aspects of its culture."

Like all definitions, the above requires amplification to make its implications clear. Its crux lies in the phrase "conscious, organized effort." All societies seek to perpetuate their own cultures, but they usually do this unconsciously and as a part of the normal processes of individual training and socialization. Conscious, organized efforts to pereptuate a culture can arise only when a society becomes conscious that there are cultures other than its own and that the existence of its own culture is threatened. Such consciousness, in turn, is a by-product of close and continuous contact with other societies;

an acculturation phenomenon under the definition developed by the above-mentioned committee.

The phrase "selected aspects of its culture" also requires elaboration. Nativistic movements concern themselves with particular elements of culture, never with cultures as wholes. This generalization holds true whether we regard cultures as continuums of long duration or follow the usual ethnographic practice of applying the term "a culture" to the content of such a continuum at a particular point in time. The avowed purpose of a nativistic movement may be either to revive the past culture or to perpetuate the current one, but it never really attempts to do either. Any attempt to revive a past phase of culture in its entirety is immediately blocked by the recognition that this phase was, in certain respects, inferior to the present one and by the incompatability of certain past culture patterns with current conditions. Even the current phase of a culture is never satisfactory at all points and also includes a multitude of elements which seem too trivial to deserve deliberate perpetuation. What really happens in all nativistic movements is that certain current or remembered elements of culture are selected for emphasis and given symbolic value. The more distinctive such elements are with respect to other cultures with which the society is in contact, the greater their potential value as symbols of the society's unique character.

The main considerations involved in this selective process seem to be those of distinctiveness and of the practicability of reviving or perpetuating the element under current conditions. Thus the Ghost Dance laid great stress on the revival of such distinctive elements of Indian culture as games and ceremonial observances, elements which could be revived under agency conditions. At the same time it allowed its adherent to continue the use of cloth, guns, kettles and other objects of European manufacture which were obviously superior to their aboriginal equivalents. In fact, in many cases the converts were assured that when the dead returned and the whites were swept away, the houses, cattle and other valuable property of the whites would remain for the Indians to inherit.

All the phenomena to which the term nativistic has been applied have in common these factors of selection of culture elements and deliberate, conscious effort to perpetuate such elements. However, they differ so widely in other respects that they cannot be understood without further analysis. At the outset it is necessary to distinguish between those forms of nativism which involve an attempt to revive extinct or at least moribund elements of culture and those which merely seek to perpetuate current ones. For convenience we will refer to the first of these forms as *revivalistic nativism,* to the second as *perpetuative nativism.* These two forms are not completely exclusive. Thus a revivalistic nativistic movement will be almost certain to include in its selection of elements some of those which are current in the culture although derived from its past. Conversely a perpetuative nativistic movement may include elements which had been consciously revived at an earlier date. However, the emphases of these two forms are distinct. The revivalistic type of nativism can be illustrated by such movements as the Celtic revival in Ireland, with its emphasis on the medieval Irish tradition in literature and its attempt to revive a moribund national language. The perpetuative type of nativism can be illustrated by the conditions existing in some of the Rio Grande Pueblos or in various Indian groups in Guatemala. Such groups are only vaguely conscious of their past culture and make no attempts to revive it, but they have developed elaborate and conscious techniques for the perpetuation of selected aspects of their current culture and are unalterably opposed to assimilation into the alien society which surrounds them.

There is a further necessity for distinguishing between what we may call *magical nativism* and *rational nativism.* It may well be questioned whether any sort of nativistic movement can be regarded as genuinely rational, since all such movements are, to some extent, unrealistic, but at least the movements of the latter order appear rational by contrast with those of the former.

Magical nativistic movements are often spectacular and always troublesome to administrators, facts which explain why they have received so much attention from anthropologists. Such movements are comparable in many respects to the messianic movements which have arisen in many societies in times of stress. They usually originate with some individual who assumes the role of prophet and is accepted by the people because they wish to believe. They always lean heavily on the supernatural and usually embody apocalyptic and millennial aspects. In such movements moribund elements of culture are not revived for their own sake or in anticipation of practical advantages from the elements themselves. Their revival is part of a magical formula designed to modify the society's environment in ways which will be favorable to it. The selection of elements from the past culture as tools for magical manipulation is easily explainable on the basis of their psychological associations. The society's members feel that by behaving as the ancestors did they will, in some usually undefined way, help to recreate the total situation in which the ancestors lived. Perhaps it would be more accurate to say that they are attempting to recreate those aspects of the ancestral situation which appear desirable in retrospect.

Such magical nativistic movements seem to differ from ordinary messianic and millennial movements in only two respects. In the nativistic movements the anticipated millenium is modeled directly on the past, usually with certain additions and modifications, and the symbols which are magically manipulated to bring it about are more or less familiar elements of culture to which new meanings have been attached. In non-nativistic messianic movements, the millennial condition is represented as something new and unique and the symbols manipulated to bring it about tend to be new and unfamiliar. Even in these respects the differences are none too clear. New elements of culture often emerge in connection with magical nativistic movements, as in the case of the distinctive Ghost Dance art. Conversely, messianic movements may lean heavily upon the familiar symbolism of the culture, as in the case of most Christian cults of this type. The basic feature of both messianic cults and magical nativistic movements is that they represent frankly irrational flights from reality. Their differences relate only to the ways in which such flights are implemented and are, from the point of view of their functions, matters of minor importance.

What we have chosen to call rational nativistic movements are a pheonmenon of a quite different sort. While such movements resemble the magical ones in their conscious effort to revive or perpetuate selected elements of culture, they have different motivations. What these are can be understood more readily if we reintroduce at this point the distinction previously made between revivalistic and perpetuative nativistic movements. Rational revivalistic nativistic movements are, almost without exception, associated with frustrating situations and are primarily attempts to compensate for the frustrations of the society's members. The elements revived become symbols of a period when the society was free or, in retrospect, happy or great. Their usage is not magical but psychological. By keeping the past in mind, such elements help to reestablish and maintain the self respect of the group's members in the face of adverse conditions. Rational perpetuative nativistic movements, on the other hand, find their main function in the maintenance of social solidarity. The elements selected for perpetuation become symbols of the society's existence as a unique entity. They provide the society's members with a fund of common knowledge and experience which is exclusively their own and which sets them off from the members of other societies. In both types of rational nativistic movement the culture elements selected for symbolic use are chosen realistically and with regard to the possibility of perpetuating them under current conditions.

It must be emphasized that the four forms of nativistic movement just discussed are not absolutes. Purely revivalistic or perpetuative, magical or rational movements form a very small minority of the observed cases. However, these forms represent the polar positions of series within which all or nearly all nativistic movements can be placed. Moreover, it will usually be found that a given nativistic movement lies much closer to one end of such a scale than to the other if it is analyzed in terms of the criteria used to establish the polar positions. If we combine the polar positions in the two series, the result is a fourfold typology of nativistic movements, as follows:

1. Revivalistic-magical   3. Perpetuative-magical
2. Revivalistic-rational   4. Perpetuative-rational

Forms 1, 2, and 4 in this typology recur with great frequency, while form 3 is so rare that the writer has been unable to find any clearly recognizable example of it. The reason for this probably lies in the conditions which are usually responsible for magical nativistic movements. The inception of such movements can be traced almost without exception to conditions of extreme hardship or at least extreme dissatisfaction with the status quo. Since the current culture is associated with such conditions and has failed to ameliorate them, magical efficacy in modifying these conditions can scarcely be ascribed to any of its elements. Nevertheless, a perpetuative-magical movement might very well arise in the case of a society which currently occupies an advantageous position but sees itself threatened with an imminent loss of that position. It is highly probable that if we could canvass the whole range of nativistic movements examples of this type could be found.

An understanding of the various contact situations in which nativistic movements may arise is quite as necessary for the study of these phenomena as is a typology of such movements. There have been many cases of contact in which they have not arisen at all. The reasons for this seem to be so variable and in many cases so obscure that nothing like a satisfactory analysis is possible. The most that we can say is that nativistic movements are unlikely to arise in situations where both societies are satisfied with their current relationship, or where societies which find themselves at a disadvantage can see that their condition is improving. However, such movements may always be initiated by particular individuals or groups who stand to gain by them and, if the prestige of such initiators is high enough, may achieve considerable followings even when there has been little previous dissatisfaction.

Although the immediate causes of nativistic movements are highly variable, most of them have as a common denominator a situation of inequality between the societies in contact. Such inequalities may derive either from the attitudes of the societies involved or from actual situations of dominance and submission. In order to understand the motives for nativistic movements the distinction between these two sources of inequality must be kept clearly in mind. Inequality based on attitudes of superiority and inferiority may exist in the absence of real dominance, although situations of dominance

seem to be uniformly accompanied by the development of such attitudes. As regards attitudes of superiority and inferiority, two situations
may exist. Each of the groups involved in the contact may consider
itself superior or one group may consider itself superior with the other
acquiescing in its own inferiority. There seem to be no cases in which
each of the groups involved in a contact considers itself inferior. The
nearest approach to such a condition is the recognition of mixed
inferiority and superiority, i.e., the members of each group regard
their own culture as superior in certain respects and inferior in others.
Such a condition is especially favorable to the processes of culture
exchange and ultimate assimilation of the two groups. It rarely if
ever results in the development of nativistic movements.

The type of situation in which each society considers itself superior
is well illustrated by the relations between Mexicans and Indians in
our own Southwest. In this case factors of practical dominance are
ruled out by the presence of a third group, the Anglo-American, which
dominates Indian and Mexican alike. Although the two subject
groups are in close contact, each of them feels that any assimilation
would involve a loss of prestige. The transfer of individuals from
one social-cultural continuum to the other is met by equal resistance
on both sides and the processes of assimilation never have a chance
to get under way. Under such circumstances the life of each of the
societies involved becomes a perpetuative-rational nativistic movement. Each group is conscious of its own culture and consciously
seeks to perpetuate its distinctive elements. At the same time this
consciousness of difference is devoid of envy or frustration and produces no friction. The members of each group pursue their own goals
with the aid of their own techniques and, although the situation does
not preclude economic rivalries, witness the constant quarrels over
water rights, it does preclude social rivalries. It seems that the establishment of such attitudes of mutual social exclusiveness, without
hatred or dominance, provides the soundest basis for organizing
symbiotic relationships between societies and should be encouraged
in all cases where the attitudes of one or both of the groups in contact preclude assimilation.

Contact situations comparable to that just discussed are not infrequent but they seem to be less common than those in which both groups agree on the superiority of one of the parties. It must be repeated that such attitudes are not necessarily linked with conditions of actual dominance. Thus the Japanese during the early period of European contact acquiesced in the European's estimate of his own superiority and borrowed European culture elements eagerly and indiscriminately although maintaining national independence. Again, the disunited German states of the eighteenth century acknowledged the superiority of French culture and were eager for French approval even when no political factors were involved.

When two groups stand in such a mutually recognized relationship of superiority and inferiority, but with no factors of actual dominance involved, the contact will rarely if ever give rise to nativistic movements of the magical type. The relationship cannot produce the extreme stresses which drive the members of a society into such flights from reality. On the other hand, the contact may well give rise to rational nativistic movements, but these will rarely if ever appear during the early contact period. At first the superior group is usually so sure of its position that it feels no reluctance toward borrowing convenient elements from the culture of the inferior one. Conversely, the inferior group borrows eagerly from the superior one and looks forward to full equality with it as soon as the cultural differences have been obliterated. During this period impecunious members of the superior group are likely to turn their prestige to practical advantage by marrying rich members of the inferior one and, for a time, genuine assimilation appears to be under way. In such a situation the nativistic trends will normally appear first in the superior group, which is naturally jealous of its prestige. The movements inaugurated will generally be of the perpetuative-rational type, designed to maintain the status quo, and will include increasing reluctance to borrow elements of culture from the inferior group and the increase of social discrimination against its members and those of the superior group who consort with them.

When such a nativistic movement gets well under way in the superior group, there will usually be a nativistic response from the inferior one. Finding themselves frustrated in their desire for equality, with or without actual assimilation, the inferiors will develop their own nativistic movements, acting on the well-known sour grapes principle. However, these movements will be of the rivalistic-rational rather than the perpetuative-rational type. The culture elements selected for emphasis will tend to be drawn from the past rather than the present, since the attitudes of the superior group toward the current culture will have done much to devaluate it. In general, symbolic values will be attached, by preference, to culture elements which were already on the wane at the time of the first contact with the superior group, thus embodying in the movement a denial that the culture of the other group ever was considered superior.

We have already said that attitudes of superiority and inferiority seem to be present in all cases of contact involving actual dominance. Combining these two sets of factors we get the following possible situations for contact groups:

1. Dominant-superior   3. Dominated-superior
2. Dominant-inferior   4. Dominated-inferior

These situations assume agreement on the part of the groups involved not only with respect to dominance, readily demonstrable, but also with respect to attitudes. The frequent lack of such agreement makes it necessary to add a fifth situation, that in which the dominant and dominated group each considers itself superior. The other possible combinations, those involving attitudes of inferiority on the part of both dominant and dominated and those involving attitudes of mixed inferiority and superiority on both sides, may be ruled out from the present discussion. The first of these possible combinations simply does not occur. The second occurs rather frequently but, as in the cases where it occurs without domination, normally results in assimilation rather than the production of nativistic movements.

The idea that nativistic movements may arise in dominant as well as dominated groups appears strange to us since most of our experience of such movements comes from the contact of Europeans with native peoples. However, we must not forget that Europeans have occupied a singularly favored position in such contacts. Even where the European settles permanently among a native population, he remains a mere outlier of white society and, thanks to modern means of transportation and communication, can keep close touch with the parent body. This parent body is shielded from contact and assimilation and is thus able to send out to its colonial ruling groups constant increments of individuals who are culturally unmixed. Moreover, the technological superiority of European culture has, until recently, rendered the dominance of colonial groups secure. The nativism of Europeans has, therefore, been largely unconscious and entirely of the perpetuative-rational type. It has manifested itself in such things as the practice of sending children back to Europe to be educated or the Englishman's insistence on dressing for dinner even when alone in a remote outpost of empire. Most dominant groups have been less fortunate. They have found themselves threatened, from the moment of their accession to power, not only by foreign invasion or domestic revolt but also by the insidious processes of assimilation which might, in the long run, destroy their distinctive powers and privileges. This threat was especially menacing when, as in most of the pre-machine-age empires, the dominant and dominated groups differed little if at all in physical type. Among such rulers the frustrations which motivate nativistic movements in inferior or dominated groups were replaced by anxieties which produced very much the same results.

Returning to the contact situations previously tabulated, we find that dominant-superior groups tend to initiate perpetuative-rational forms of nativism as soon as they achieve power and to adhere to them with varying intensity as long as they remain in power. Thus the various groups of nomad invaders who conquered China all attempted to maintain much of their distinctive culture and at the height of their power they issued repressive measures directed not only against the Chinese but also against those of their own group who had begun to adopt Chinese culture. It seems probable that revivalist-rational forms of nativism will not arise in a dominant-superior group, at least as regards elements of culture which were moribund at the time of their accession to power, although this form of nativism might develop with respect to culture elements which had fallen into neglect during the period of power. It seems possible also that, under conditions of extreme threat, some form of brief revivalist-magical nativism might arise in such a group, but information that might verify these conjectures is lacking.

The situation in which a dominant group acknowledges its cultural inferiority to the dominated is one which must arise very infrequently. However, examples of it are provided by such cases as that of the Goths at the time of their conquest of Italy. Such a group immediately finds itself caught on the horns of a dilemma. It can remove its feelings of inferiority only by undergoing cultural if not social assimilation with the conquered society, while such assimilation is almost certain to cost it its dominant position. It seems probable that such a society might develop nativistic movements either when its desire for cultural assimilation with the conquered was frustrated or when it found its dominant position seriously threatened, but again information is lacking.

There is abundant information on nativistic movements among dominated groups and in discussing these we stand on firm ground. A dominated group which considers itself superior will normally develop patterns of rational nativism from the moment that it is brought under domination. These patterns may be either revivalist or perpetuative but are most likely to be a combination of both. One of the commonest rationalizations for loss of a dominant position is that it is due to a society's failure to adhere closely enough to its distinctive culture patterns. Very often such nativism will acquire a semi-magical quality founded on the belief that if the group will only stand firm and maintain its individuality it will once again become dominant. Fully developed magical-revivalist nativism is also very likely to appear in groups of this sort since to the actual deprivations entailed by subjection there are added the frustrations involved by loss of dominance. These frustrations are somewhat mitigated in the cases where the dominant group recognizes the superiority of the dominated group's culture. Such attitudes strengthen the rational nativistic tendencies of the dominated group and diminish the probabilities for magical-revivalist nativism of the more extreme type. Lastly, in cases where the dominant group concurs with the dominated in considering certain aspects of the latter's culture superior but will not grant the superiority of the culture as a whole, this attitude will stimulate the dominated group to focus attention upon such aspects of its culture and endow them with added symbolic value.

A dominated group which considers itself inferior, a condition common among societies of low culture which have recently been brought under European domination, is extremely unlikely to develop any sort of rational nativism during the early period of its subjection. It may, however, develop nativism of the revivalist-magical type if it is subjected to sufficient hardships. The threshold of suffering at which such movements may develop will vary greatly from group to group and will be influenced not only by the degree of hardship but also by the society's patterns of reliance upon the supernatural. A devout society will turn to nativism of this sort long before a skeptical one will. If the hardships arising from subjection are not extreme, the inferior group will usually show great eagerness to assume the culture of the dominant society, this eagerness being accompanied by a devaluation of everything pertaining to its own. Nativistic movements tend to arise only when the members of the subject society find that their assumption of the culture of the dominant group is being effectively opposed by it, or that it is not improving their social position. The movements which originate under these circumstances are practically always rational with a combination of revivalist and perpetuative elements. In this respect they resemble the nativistic movements which originate in inferior groups which are not subject to domination and there can be little doubt that the primary causes are the same in both cases. These movements are a response to frustration rather than hardship and would not arise if the higher group were willing to assimilate the lower one.

Rational nativistic movements can readily be converted into mechanisms for aggression. Since the dominated society has been frustrated in its earlier desires to become acculturated and to achieve social equality, it can frustrate the dominant society in turn by refusing to accept even those elements of culture which the dominant group is eager to share with it. Dominated societies which have acquired these attitudes and developed conscious techniques for preventing further acculturation present one of the most difficult problems for administrators. Passive resistance requires much less energy than any of the techniques needed to break it down, especially if the culture patterns of the dominant group preclude the use of forcible methods.

One final aspect of nativistic movements remains to be considered. The generalizations so far developed have been based upon the hypothesis that societies are homogeneous and react as wholes to contact situations. Very frequently this is not the case, especially in societies which have a well-developed class organization. In such societies nativistic tendencies will be strongest in those clases or individuals who occupy a favored position and who feel this position threatened by culture change. This factor may produce a split in the society, the favored individuals or groups indulging in a rational nativism, either revivalistic or perpetuative, while those in less-favored positions are eager for assimilation. This condition can be observed in many immigrant groups in America where individuals who enjoyed high status in the old European society attempt to perpetuate the patterns of that society while those who were of low status do their best to become Americanized.

In a rapidly shrinking world the study of nativistic movements, as of acculturation in general, has ceased to be a matter of purely academic interest. As contacts between societies become more frequent and more general, the need for an understanding of the potentialities of such contact situations becomes more urgent. The troubles which they usually involve can be traced, with few exceptions, to two factors: exploitation and frustration. The first of these is the easier to deal with and may well disappear with the spread of modern science and techniques to all parts of the world. The second is more difficult to deal with since its removal entails fundamental changes in attitudes of superiority and inferiority. Without these there would be no bar to the assimilation of societies in contact situations or to the final creation of a world society. However, this seems to be one of those millennial visions mentioned elsewhere in this report. Failing assimilation, the happiest situation which can arise out of the contact of two societies seems to be that in which each society is firmly convinced of its own superiority. Rational revivalistic or perpetuative nativistic movements are the best mechanism which has so far been developed for establishing these attitudes in groups whose members suffer from feelings of inferiority. It would appear, therefore, that they should be encouraged rather than discouraged.

The essay which we have entitled "Culture Transfer and Acculturation" represents excerpts from the last three chapters of Acculturation in Seven American Indian Tribes, *edited by Ralph Linton (Appleton-Century, 1940). The two final chapters, originally entitled "The Process of Culture Tranfser" and "The Distinctive Aspects of Acculturation," and written by Linton, not only are conclusions to that volume but they also sum up his thinking on the process of culture change, the reaction of societies to new and foreign elements, and the diverse aspects of the acculturation process which are important in understanding his thought in* The Tree of Culture.

Culture Transfer and Acculturation

❖ Culture change always involves not only the adoption of new culture elements but their modification in form or meaning or both, and also modifications in the pre-existing culture. The latter may include the elimination of certain elements but need not necessarily do so. In the acceptance of a new element certain stages are recognizable irrespective of whether the new thing originated within the sociocultural configuration or was borrowed from another group. It is taken up first by a single individual or small group of individuals; the innovators, who are for some reason dissatisfied with the status quo. These innovators anticipate advantage from the new thing, but this advantage may be in terms of practical utility, or prestige, or both. From the innovators the new element may or may not spread to other members of the society, their acceptance or rejection of it being determined by considerations of advantage similar to those operative in the case of the innovators. Dissemination of the new thing to the total society is not necessary for its successful incorporation into the culture and its spread is, in practice, limited to the members of certain socially established categories of persons as adult men, nobles, etc. Dissemination of the new thing may be followed either by rejection, if it fails to show superiority to the old element or elements which it might replace, or by acceptance, with progressive modifications both in it and in the culture matrix. These processes of modification run concurrently with those of dissemination, and their success is of the greatest importance for the final and complete acceptance of the new thing. Under normal conditions culture change involves duplication of function but no interruption in the satisfaction of the group's needs. It can, therefore, be accomplished without disorganization and with no more discomfort to the individual than is involved in changing pre-existing habits. . . .

We will now turn to the additional factors and processes which are present in a particular aspect of culture change, i.e., that of culture transfer as a result of contact between two groups. There appear to be certain phenomena which are universally associated with culture transfer and which provide a background without which the variations observable in specific cases cannot be understood.

It seems best at the very outset to dispose of one factor frequently present in situations of contact and culture transfer. This is the factor of racial differences between the groups involved. The associations which the groups themselves come to attach to these differences may be of considerable importance in determining their behavior and attitudes toward each other, but it seems to be the associations rather than the differences which are significant. Racial differences are no bar to the amalgamation of two groups through intermarriage. In fact, open or illicit interbreeding is one of the commonest of contact phenomena and the offspring of such unions have never proved to be inferior in any respect to the parent stocks. As regards the transfer of culture from one group to another, all our present information seems to indicate that any race can assume any type of culture given a full opportunity to do so. . . . Actually, we know that in the past culture elements of the most homogeneous sort have been diffused over great areas and accepted and assimilated by groups of widely different races. . . .

Factors other than those of practical utility or even of compatibility with the pre-existing culture configuration may be of great importance in determining whether a new thing will be accepted. The auspices under which novelties are presented to the group and the associations which come to be attached to them in consequence have a profound effect on their potentialities for conferring prestige upon those who accept them. It is at this point that the origin of new culture elements becomes significant for understanding subsequent developments. If the novelty originates within the group, its associations will derive primarily from the prestige status of the innovators. If it originates outside the group, its associations will derive not only from the innovators but also from the donor society. In other words, the attitudes of the receiving group toward the donor group will attach themselves, at least initially, to the elements of culture which contact between the two groups makes available for borrowing. Since it is a demonstrable fact that most cultures owe a large part of their content to borrowing, these attitudes are a factor in many situations of culture change. . . .

Enough cases of culture transfer have been observed to make it clear that the borrowing of elements is much more frequent than that of trait complexes, but the reason for this is still uncertain. The number of elements in any culture is vastly greater than the number of functional complexes, making their transfer much more probable on a purely chance basis. The adoption of single elements and their integration into pre-existing complexes also involves less modification in the culture of borrowers than does the taking over of whole new complexes. Lastly, in many contact situations it may be easier for members of the borrowing group to perceive and imitate certain items in the culture of the donors than for them to apprehend the total complexes of which these items are a part. . . .

It seems that, other things being equal, certain sorts of culture elements are more readily transferable than others. Tangible objects such as tools, utensils, or ornaments are taken over with great ease, in fact they are usually the first things transferred in contact situations. . . . The transfer of patterns of behavior is more difficult. It requires at least face-to-face contact over a period long enough to enable one group to observe the activities of the other and does not always result even then. The transfer of elements which lack concreteness and ready observability of objects and overt behavior is the most difficult of all. It requires not only face-to-face contact but also the presence of some means of communication adequate for the conveyance of abstractions. In general, the more abstract the element the more difficult the transfer. . . . The common element in this range of variation seems to be that of the relative ease with which the foreign element of culture can be perceived by members of the borrowing group. Objects can be perceived most easily, culture elements of other sorts with progressive difficulty.

The perception of culture elements by the borrowers is, obviously, the first step in their transfer. However, the most easily perceived aspect of a culture element, even such an abstract one as a story, is its form. Its meaning to members of the donor society can only be conveyed by elaborate explanations and not always then, for the most important meanings attached to many acts and objects are often imperfectly formulated and poorly verbalized. . . . The result is that most culture elements are transferred in terms of their objective form stripped of the meaning which is an integral part of them in their original context. At most they may carry over vague associations . . . derived from the observed behavior and attitudes of the donor group in connection with them. Their primary meaning, as far as the receiving group is concerned, will be what they derive from the single fact of their original association with the donor group. . . .

It is safe to say that no society, so long as it exists as a distinct entity, will take over even the purely objective aspects of an alien culture *in toto*. It will pick out certain things from the range of those made available for borrowing and accept these while remaining indifferent or even actively opposed to others. In the presence of long contact, indifference and opposition may be progressively broken down, and under such circumstances the selective factor expresses itself in terms of sequence adoption, certain things being taken over before others.

Aside from the factor of relative ease of perception of culture elements of different orders, the considerations involved in their selection and adoption seem to be fundamentally the same as those

128

involved in the dissemination of culture elements within the group. New things are borrowed on the basis of their utility, compatibility with pre-existing culture patterns, and prestige associations. All three of these are, of course, variables and the outcome of exposure to a new culture element will depend upon a very intricate combination of them. The possible ranges of variation in utility and compatibility are fairly obvious, but the importance of prestige is frequently overlooked. Although elements in foreign cultures are perceived objectively, certain more or less irrational associations with them are present from the start. The most important of these are the associations derived from their identification with the donor group. These are qualified, in some cases, by the donor group's attitudes toward these elements of their culture, in so far as these can be perceived by the borrowers. Thus if a respected foreign group apparently attaches great importance to some custom, say wearing clothes or sitting on chairs, the borrowing group will feel that this custom must have some advantages which are not obvious and be that much more eager to take it over. The prestige potentialities of borrowed culture elements will depend primarily upon the attitude of the borrowers toward the donors. . . . If one group admires another, they will go to a great deal of trouble and inconvenience to be like them, while if they despise them they will put up with a good deal of trouble and inconvenience not to be like them. The tropical native who begins to wear clothes and replaces his cool thatched roof with corrugated iron because he sees Europeans do these things, and the European in the tropics who keeps his stiff collars in spite of the temperature are cases in point. . . .

The attachment of such values seems to be largely chance determined. Other things being equal, the order of selection of borrowed elements is probably controlled primarily by considerations of utility and of compatibility with the pre-existing culture of the borrowers.

The acceptance and successful integration of certain culture elements may facilitate the acceptance of others which have been functionally related to them in the donor's culture. Thus the acceptance of agricultural machinery would obviously be made easier by a previous acceptance of agriculture. In fact, it would be impossible without it. At the same time, we have seen that trait complexes may be borrowed as wholes, and we have no proof that the acceptance of certain elements is constantly or even usually followed by the acceptance of others which were originally related to them. Borrowed elements, even when they retain their original form with little modification, may be put to quite new uses by the borrowers and may acquire associations very different from those which they had in their original context. In such cases it is an open quetsion whether their presence has any influence on the borrowing of originally related elements. The number of factors which affect borrowing is so large and the variation in the factors themselves so great that it seems probable that no significant generalizations can be made on this particular point.

Another interesting aspect of culture borrowing is the problem of the minimum time required for the full acceptance and integration of new elements. We know that this process requires time and it seems certain that some new things require more time than others. One might suspect that this time factor would be correlated in some way with the extent of the modifications in both the new element and the pre-existing culture necessary to its successful integration. However, we know that modifications of several sorts may go on simultaneously. All we can say is that under optimum conditions the transfer of a culture element can be accomplished with surprising speed, as when an entire group becomes conscious of the advantages of writing and practically all its members learn to read and write within a few months. This happened among the Cherokee after the invention of Sequoia's syllabary, and in certain of the Polynesian Islands under missionary encouragement. It is interesting to note in this connection the speed with which new societies and cultures can be synthesized from diverse elements once these have been brought together. Thus the life of cattlemen in the old West presented all the phenomena of a distinct culture, yet its development, flowering, and final dissolution took place within a period of about sixty years. . . .

Enough situations of contact and borrowing have been observed to make two points clear. First, borrowing is normally a reciprocal process, and second, its logical, although by no means always its actual, end product is the amalgamation of the two cultures involved, resulting in a new culture differing in certain respects from either of its parent cultures.

Evidence for the reciprocal nature of borrowing is afforded by all cases in which two groups of diverse culture have been in contact for any length of time. However, the extent of borrowing by each of the two groups involved will usually be different, one taking over more than the other. At least two factors are operative in determining the differential in culture transfer. One of these is the relative effectiveness of the techniques for adaptation to the local environment which each culture provides. To cite a concrete example, Europeans in the Arctic have borrowed very heavily from the Eskimo, copying their clothing, housing, hunting methods, and even, to a considerable degree, their food habits. These elements of culture represent successful adaptations to a type of environment alien to normal European experience and with which the established patterns of European culture cannot cope successfully. . . .

The other factor is that of relative prestige. Other things being equal, a group which recognizes its social inferiority will borrow more extensively from its superiors than the superiors will borrow from it. However, considerations of superiority and inferiority are never strong enough to prevent some transfer upward. This process is facilitated by the tendency, already mentioned, for groups of different status in contact situations to single out certain elements of culture as focal points for prestige associations. The superior group will cling to these even in the face of considerable discomfort and may even forcibly exclude the inferior group from participating in them. At the same time, elements of the superior culture to which no such associations have become attached may be eliminated and replaced by new elements borrowed from the inferior group. Thus the European in West Africa clings to the full clothing which his ancestors developed in a sub-Arctic environment, but has changed his food habits in the native direction, adopting such delectable dishes as palm oil chop without any sense of losing caste. What actually happens under such conditions of mutual transfer will, therefore, depend upon the utility and prestige factors.

In the current interchanges of culture between European and non-European groups, the process of culture exchange is never carried through to its logical conclusion. The complete amalgamation of two cultures has as its inseparable accompaniment the complete amalgamation of the two societies involved. As long as these retain their separate identity their cultures will retain certain differences. . . . In most cases the process of culture exchange results not in the production of a new, homogeneous culture but in the synthesis of two new cultures with mutual adaptations which permit the societies which bear them to live together in a symbiotic relationship.

All culture transfer has as its prerequisite contact between the groups involved, and the nature of this contact is one of the factors influencing the whole process. However, before going into this, something should be said of the influence of contact on culture change in general. The fact of contact in itself increases the force of the external and internal stimuli toward culture change which are constantly present. From the moment of its appearance the contacting group introduces new factors into the general environment. In all but a few extreme cases of isolation, the environment of a given society includes not only natural phenomena but also other societies. Even sporadic contacts with a new group influence relations with the groups previously present. If desirable articles are obtained from the newcomers, trade with groups which did not have similar contact will be stimulated, or the added possibilities of loot will increase the contacting group's danger from attack. If the newcomers are hostile, their presence will be a strong stimulus to alliance with groups already known. If they are friendly, the possibility of obtaining help from them will increase the contacting group's truculence toward its neighbors. In brief, the appearance of a new group always leads to realignments and changes in the relations of those already present, with a consequent need for cultural adaptations.

Such contacts also lead almost inevitably to alterations in the natural environment or at least to changes in its potentialities for the resident group. Even if the newcomers are only transient traders, they will be in search of and exchange valuable objects for certain products and not others. These products may previously have played only an unimportant role in the native economy. Contrast the importance of rubber to a native tribe who used it only for the mouth-pieces of blow guns with the importance the same material assumed when it was discovered that it could be exchanged for tools, beads, and cloth. Again, the small fur-bearing animals which played a minor role in the economy of the Canadian Indians before White contact rose to major importance immediately thereafter. Under such conditions new and more intensive methods of exploitation will be developed with an ultimate reduction of the supply and an upset in the natural ecology which may have far-reaching consequences. If the newcomers actually settle in the region, their presence will result in a diminution of resources for the groups already there or even, in extreme cases, in the complete elimination of resources of a certain sort. The destruction of the buffalo by White hunters cut the very foundation from under the cultures of the Plains tribes and contributed more to their subjugation than all the White soldiers.

The society must modify its culture to meet these new environmental conditions if it is to survive. At the same time, the fact of contact has profound psychological effects upon the society's members. It goes without saying that any marked maladjustment of the group to its environment will be reflected in individual discomforts and consequent discontent, but the effects of contact are of a more direct sort. Under ordinary circumstances the average individual is no more conscious of the culture in which he participates than he is of the air he breathes. The discomforts and thwartings which its particular patterns impose upon him are accepted as inevitable, much as we accept the fact of a hot summer or a rainy day. The presence of another group with a different set of habits and values makes him culture conscious, and it is a short step from this to a critical attitude toward the institutions of his own society. He may disapprove of much of the newcomers' behavior, but at the same time he will envy them some of their liberties. . . .

The presence of newcomers also arouses the curiosity of individuals and provides opportunities for novel experience. All explorers can testify to the extreme interest that most natives take in everything that the visitors have and do. If the new experiences prove pleasurable, the members of the group develop new desires whose satisfaction calls for change in the familiar routine. A man may have to hunt twice as hard as he did before or indulge in some new form of labor in order to get whiskey for the occasional sprees which, once experienced, become the high point of existence. To sum up, contact even without the transfer of culture elements, if such a thing is possible, is a strong stimulus to culture change. It not only modifies the environment but also makes the individual critical of the *status quo* and more receptive to novelties.

The range of possible forms of contact between groups is enormous. In fact, no two cases of contact are identical in all their aspects. Contacts may vary in duration, in closeness, and in continuity, all three of these variables operating independently, but it is an open question how significant any or all these factors are in influencing the processes of culture change. It seems that, at most, they impose certain limits upon the possibility of culture borrowing. Thus obviously there will be more chance for culture exchange under conditions of long, close, and continuous contact than under conditions of brief and distant contact. However, in the matter of culture transfer the old adage that you can lead a horse to water but you can't make him drink is very much to the point. Some of the small religious communities in the eastern United States, for example certain Pennsylvania German sects, have been in close and continuous contact with other Americans since the eighteenth century, yet their cultural borrowings have been highly selective and the number of elements taken over relatively small. On the other hand, the Japanese, whose contact with Europeans has been much briefer and immeasurably less close in terms of space, have borrowed much more extensively and, apparently, with much less discrimination. Again, how are we to evaluate the rather frequent cases of discontinuous contacts which are close while they last? For example, whalers makng seasonal visits to the Arctic often live on terms of the closest intimacy with Eskimo groups during the few months they are there. The Eskimos have the run of the ship and the Whites take temporary Eskimo wives. Are the chances for culture transfer better or worse in such a case than they are in that of a small colony of European administratiors living year in and year out among natives whom they keep at arm's length?

Apparently the really significant features of contact as influencing culture transfer are not duration, closeness, and continuity, but the effects of the contact on the pre-existing environment, the elements of culture which it makes available for borrowing, and the attitudes which it engenders between the two groups involved. . . .

The elements of culture which are available for borrowing represent a variable which is obviously of great importance in determining the culture transfers which may take place in contact situations. It has already been pointed out that no one individual is ever familiar with the total culture of his society and that the knowledge and activities included in that culture are divided among the society's members according to its patterns of organization. . . . In the more complex cultures this division is often carried to great lengths. In contact situations it seems to be rather exceptional for the contacting groups to be fully representative of their respective societies. . . .

The attitudes which may exist between groups which are in contact are as complex as those which may exist between individuals and as difficult to classify under such simple terms as hostility or friendship, admiration or contempt. There are all sorts of ambivalences and also differential attitudes toward the other group's abilities along various lines. Thus one tribe may despise another for the freedom of behavior it allows its women while admiring it for the courage of its men. Again, two groups may live for generations under alternating conditions of hostility and alliance against a common enemy.

It is particularly important in this connection to note that overt hostility, i.e., actual warfare, seems to impose very little bar to culture borrowing. . . . Conditions of warfare may even be more favorable to culture transfer than those of peace. Objects from the enemy groups are obtained as loot and subsequently imitated in native manufacture, war practices are observed and copied, while the taking of captives with their subsequent incorporation into their captor's society through slavery, concubinage, or adoption establishes the optimum conditions for culture transfer.

Again, the fact that one group has conquered another by force of arms does not necessarily imply that the conquerors will despise the conquered. They may even recognize their superiority in everything but warfare and be eager to borrow from them, clinging only to those elements of their original culture which have become symbolic of their dominant position. . . .

Lastly, there is the factor of the attitude of the dominant group toward cultural borrowing on the part of the dominated one. If they see in such borrowing a threat to their own social position or actual power, they will do their best to prevent it and, if their domination is strong enough, may be successful with respect to certain elements. Thus there are many parts of the world in which the Whites have successfully prevented the diffusion of modern firearms to the native population, others in which they have successfully discouraged the diffusion of White clothing or furniture. In the first case, the practical considerations involved are obvious. The worse armed the natives, the poorer their chances of revolt. In the second case the consideration is purely one of prestige. It is felt that when the native assumes European costume he narrows the social gap which the dominant group wishes to retain intact.

If one can generalize at all about the results of attitudes in contact situations, it would seem that the conditions least favorable for culture transfer were those which arise when a conquered group remains hostile and unreconciled but without hope of successful revolt. Under such circumstances the hostility expresses itself in terms of passive resistance and uncooperativeness. . . . This condition results in a sort of blanket opposition to the acceptance of any new elements of culture beyond those necessary to continued existence. . . .

There are two other factors present in contact situations which may be of some importance in determining their outcome. These are the relative size of the groups involved and the relative complexity of the cultures involved. Unfortunately, we have not sufficient information on the results of either of these factors to make any generalizations safe. The assumption that, when a large and a small group are

136

brought into contact, the small group will borrow more extensively than the large one cannot either be proved or disproved at present. However, there seems to be no intrinsic reason why this should be the case. A hundred individuals can learn a new thing as readily as one. That this assumption has been made so frequently is probably due to an unconscious confusion between physical and cultural factors. When a large and a small group fuse biologically, the physical type of the larger will tend to be dominant in the resultant mixed group, but it does not follow that its culture type will tend to be dominant in the resultant mixed culture.

The problem of the relative complexity of the cultures involved as affecting the outcome of culture contacts is an extremely complicated one involving first of all a clearer understanding of what constitutes culture complexity than we have at present. All cultures are complex in certain of their aspects, simple in others. Thus White technology is complex, White family organization extraordinarily simple, by contrast with the complexes of most other societies. It is safe to say that in culture transfer complex elements do not uniformly tend to replace simple ones; in fact any very high degree of complexity probably increases the difficulty of individual learning and thus makes the transfer harder. The most that we can say at present is that more complex technologies, if they provide a better control of the environment, will tend to supersede simple ones. However, the significant thing in such cases is not the greater complexity but the greater efficiency. The modern Indian prefers the auto to the horse not because it is more complicated but because it covers more ground in less time. . . .

"Acculturation comprehends those phenomena which result when groups of individuals having different cultures come into continuous first-hand contact, with subsequent changes in the original culture patterns of either or both groups." Under this definition acculturation must include the general processes operative in all cases of group contact and culture change. . . .

Most of the phenomena which have continuous first-hand contact as a prerequisite can be grouped under one or the other of two heads:

(1) those associated with directed culture change; and (2) those associated with socio-cultural fusion. . . .

The term "directed culture change" is not altogether satisfactory, but its alternative, "enforced culture change," is still less so. There is enforced change whenever modifications in a society's environment make modifications in its culture necessary to survival. Directed culture change will be taken to refer to those situations in which one of the groups in contact interferes actively and purposefully with the culture of the other. This interference may take the form of stimulating the acceptance of new culture elements, inhibiting the exercise of pre-existing culture patterns, or, as seems to be most frequently the case, doing both simultaneously. Thus the Spaniards in Mexico compelled the Indians both to attend Christian rites and to give up their own pagan rites.

The term "socio-cultural fusion" will be taken to refer to those situations in which two originally distinct cultures and societies fuse to produce a single homogeneous culture and society. The blending of Norman and Saxon elements to produce the later English would be a case in point. Genuine fusion always involves not only the disappearance of the two original cultures but also the amalgamation of the two societies through the biological process of interbreeding. Practically all cases of the so-called assimilation of one group by another group could be more accurately classed as examples of fusion, since the culture of the assimilating group is usually modified by the introduction of elements from that of the assimilated. . . .

The processes of directed culture change can only operate in those contact situations in which there is dominance and submission. Nativistic movements also appear to be rather closely correlated with this condition. The processes of fusion, on the other hand, may operate under conditions of either dominance and submission or equality. The processes of directed culture change seem to be most active and their results most obvious during the early period of a continuous first-hand contact. Nativistic movements apparently tend to appear somewhat later; at least we have no examples in which they have developed at the beginning of a contact period. In contrast, the processes of fusion usually begin at the moment of contact and continue over a long period, in some cases for many generations. Directed culture change may take place either when there is little or no tendency toward fusion or during the early stages of fusion. Conversely, fusion may take place with or without directed culture change. On the whole, there appears to be no constant or intrinsic relationship between the phenomena of these three orders, and it seems legitimate to discuss them separately.

Attitudes of dominance and submission are a very frequent, although not necessarily constant, accompaniment of continuous first-hand contact. Even when there are no factors of conquest or forceful domination, one of the contacting groups will usually recognize the superiority of the other, with a consequent eagerness to be socially and culturally identified with it. . . . Needless to say, the admired group usually concurs in the judgment of its admirers. It would be difficult to find a contact situation in which each group considers the other superior, but those in which each group considers the other inferior are not uncommon. Such attitudes make it possible for the dominant group to interfere in the normal processes of culture transfer. Even when they cannot force the inferior group to accept elements from their own culture, they can exercise what might be termed high-pressure salesmanship with respect to certain things. Conversely, elements of the inferior culture of which the superior group openly disapproves will lose their value in the eyes of the inferior group and will tend to be abandoned more readily. Thus European immigrants in this country will abandon their national costumes, or practices which are ridiculed by their American neighbors, long before they will give up other elements of culture toward which Americans are indifferent. However, as long as the pressures exerted by the dominant group are purely psychological there seems to be no serious interference with the normal processes of culture change. What would otherwise be the normal order of acceptance of borrowed elements may be interfered with, certain adoptions being given precedence over others because of the added prestige factors, but no element of culture will be eliminated until a satisfactory substitute has been found. . . .

All attempts to direct culture change are really efforts on the part of the dominant group to modify and control its own environment. The subject group is always an important part of this environment, with potentialities for furthering or impeding the aims of the dominators. Thus it is to the practical advantage of the dominant group to make the members of the inferior one perform certain services for it, or buy its goods, or stop making war on it or on other groups with which it wants to trade. It will also contribute to the peace of mind of members of the dominant group if the inferior one gives up practices which the dominant group finds repugnant. . . .

How far the dominant group will be able to change the culture of the subject one, and the methods which it can employ for the purpose will, of course, depend upon the conditions surrounding the contact. . . . The degree to which culture change can be enforced by punitive measures offers an interesting problem for investigation. It is obvious that certain forms of behavior can be inhibited and others enforced. For example, human sacrifices or war can be stopped by punishing members of the subject group who participate in them. Similarly, men of the subject group can be compelled to wear a loin cloth or women of the subject group to cover their breasts in public. In time such culture changes will become integrated with the older patterns and will be accepted by the subject group as matters of course, arousing no emotional response. However, all elements of culture which do not correspond directly to behavior lie beyond the reach of punitive measures. An individual can be punished for what he does or does not do, but he cannot be punished for what he thinks or believes. A native group can be compelled to attend church regularly but not to accept Christian doctrine. The use of force naturally arouses resentment and an added consciousness of cultural differences with, in most cases, attachment of symbolic values to many elements of the old culture. While punitive measures can unquestionably accelerate the transfer of certain culture elements, they probably delay the acceptance of many others. . . .

In all cases of directed culture change the dominant group singles out certain elements of the subject group's culture for attack and also selects certain elements of its own for imposition. This selection is, naturally, in line with the dominant group's interest and advantage. . . .

Under culture change which is both directed and enforced, the normal process of retention of old elements until satisfactory substitutes have been found is inhibited. The result is a series of losses without adequate replacements. This leaves certain of the group's needs unsatisfied, produces derangements in all sorts of social and economic relationships, and results in profound discomfort for the individuals involved.

In the contacts of Europeans with natives, the first steps in the enforcement of culture change are usually negative, i.e., certain patterns in the native culture are inhibited. War is normally the first point of attack, since it interferes with the security advantageous to trade and the exploitation of local resources. The dominant Whites ordinarily feel that if they can protect the subject group from attack they have rendered war unnecessary. However, it would be difficult to find a culture in which the functions of the war complex did not extend far beyond defense and aggression. . . . War honors may be the basis of a society's whole system of rank and social control. This situation was present among the Comanche. While warfare was still going on, the executions of individuals who stood at the top of the scale were kept in check by fear of reprisals when some men of lower rank rose above them. The end of warfare froze the system, depriving able young men of all chance of social advancement and making the old men arrogant.

Such unfortunate results follow the suppression of almost any trait complex. In Madagascar the European authorities have refused to recognize the existence of witchcraft and punish the killing of witches as murder. At the same time, they have not altered the native belief in witchcraft. The consequence has been to give the wizards carte blanche for extortion and to raise them to a dominant position in certain tribes. The general population feels helpless in the face of the new conditions. Again, the discouragement of polygyny in a society organized along those lines produces all sorts of maladjustments. In the first place, a certain number of women are prevented from getting husbands. Quite aside from personal difficulties of the sort dear to psychoanalysts, such women will be at a serious economic disadvantage. There will be no place for them in the existing economic system. Prostitution is almost certain to result with disturbing effects to the whole society. In the second place, even the women who do find husbands will suffer from the change. They will have been reared to expect companionship in the household and assistance in domestic and field labor. The necessary adaptive changes in the rest of the culture will work themselves out in time but meanwhile there will be confusion and discomfort for everyone. . . .

Examples of this sort are familiar to all students of acculturation. The only point which needs to be emphasized is that the bad results of enforced culture change probably derive as much if not more from the blocking of preexisting culture patterns as from the introduction of new ones.

The inhibition of preexisting culture patterns, with resulting lack of satisfaction for certain of the society's needs, is not a phenomenon limited to situations of directed culture change. The changes in the group's environment which are an inevitable result of the appearance of a new group or of movement into new territory have very much the same effects. Thus in the case of many of the American Indian tribes the destruction of game which resulted from the presence of Whites and the curtailment of tribal range made many of the previous techniques for obtaining food and raw materials unworkable. Conversely, a group of European peasants who settle in an American city find themselves in a new environment in which many of the techniques they brought with them are no longer effective. The problems of cleanliness and sanitation, for example, assume quite new aspects in the absence of brooks and barnyards. Such situations have in common with those of directed culture change failure of the culture to meet the needs of the group with consequent discomfort and disorganization which will continue until new techniques for meeting these needs have been developed.

Cultures are the most flexible of adaptive mechanisms. No need of a society will go unsatisfied for long. If two societies which have been brought into contact survive the shock of the initial impact, the cultures of both will soon be altered in such a way as to make it possible for them to get along together. Directed culture change is simply an effort on the part of the dominant group to make the subject group do most of the adapting to the new conditions. . . .

When two groups have achieved a working adjustment to each other and to their common natural environment, the external stimuli to further culture change are largely removed. The internal stimuli, those deriving from the discontents of individuals and their belief that conditions can be bettered, will, of course, continue in force. These will be strong enough to prevent cultural stagnation in either group and new elements developed in one will frequently be transferred to the other by the normal processes of borrowing. However, after successful mutual adaptation has been achieved, any extensive changes in the culture of either group will necessitate compensating changes in that of the other. For this reason the dominant group is usually content to let well enough alone, although it may still interfere in the culture of the subject one under certain circumstances. Its members may, for example, have altruistic feelings toward those they dominate and set about bettering their condition. Such directed culture change is usually carried on like any other, i.e., with a bland indifference to what the victims really want, and has the same results of derangement and discontent. Again the dominant group may perceive advantages to be enjoyed from some change in their subjects' habits—if, for example, they could be persuaded to wear hats or to work in factories. Lastly, the dominant group may feel that the existence of the subject group constitutes a threat to it and, if it cannot eliminate it, may make a conscious effort to assimilate it. To the last category belong the various attempts to Americanize immigrant groups and the violent attempts which have been made from time to time in Europe to destroy the distinctive cultures and languages of national minorities. However, all such cases are comparatively rare. Directed culture change is essentially a phenomenon of initial contact, becoming less strongly operative as the duration of the contact lengthens.

Let us turn now to the second group of phenomena which can be present only under conditions of continuous first hand contact; those of social-cultural fusion. It must be stressed at the outset that fusion is not a constant or necessary accompaniment of such contact. It is merely impossible in their absence. It seems that when two societies and cultures have reached a working adaptation to each other, they may exist side by side for many generations without any discernible tendency to fuse. This condition was observable in many parts of Europe before the rise of militant nationalism. For example, in Russia there were Swedish and German groups which had been there since the early eighteenth century living on amicable terms with their Russian neighbors but preserving their own language and customs. In Madagascar the Southern Sakalava are really a confederacy of three tribes all of whom recognize the same king. One of these tribes, to use the picturesque native phrase, attends to the affairs of the sea, another to the affairs of the fields, and the third to the affairs of the forest. The three groups exchange products and services and members of different tribes may even live in the same village. At the same time, each tribe has its distinctive customs. The members of other tribes know these and even regulate their behavior by them when it is courteous to do so. For example, when visiting the village of another tribe they will keep its tabus. However, they have no desire to take over such customs. Intermarriage, although not formally prohibited, is extremely rare in practice. Even when it does happen it does not break down the tribal lines, since wife and child automatically follow the customs of the husband's group.

We know that in individuals there are fundamental attitudes of security or insecurity which are deeply rooted in the personality and which influence behavior under a wide variety of circumstances. Similarly, there seem to be societies which are psychologically secure. . . . It simply never occurs to the members of such a group to envy the members of other groups or to want to be like them. It might be questioned whether such cases are not excluded from the field of acculturation study by the second half of our definition: "contact . . . with consequent changes in the original culture patterns of either or both groups." However, there is always some exchange of culture going on under these conditions, minor elements passing from one group to the other. . . . Such transfers do no more to bring about the fusion of the two groups than does our own custom of copying French styles in women's wear. The borrowed elements are modified and re-interpreted to fit their new context, while new elements appear from time to time within the cultures themselves, maintaining the distinction.

Although the circumstances under which fusion may take place are quite diverse, the actual processes of fusion are simple enough and exhibit considerable uniformity in all cases. Culture fusion begins with an exchange of elements. The factors of utility, compatibility and prestige involved in such transfers are the same as those operative in all cases of culture borrowing. So are the processes of integration into the receiving culture. The only difference is that the exchange of elements is continued long after a working adaptation of the cultures and societies involved has been reached. The stimulus to such continued borrowing seems to be primarily the desire of the group which feels itself socially inferior to become completely identified with the superior one.

It is extremely rare to find a case of fusion in which both sides have borrowed equally. The differential seems to be controlled primarily by two sets of factors, those of prestige and those of the degree of adaptation to the local environment of the two cultures involved. These factors are, of course, in constant interaction. It seems safe to say that, when both cultures represent successful adaptations to the environment, borrowing will be heavier on the side of the socially inferior group. This is in line with their greater desire for identification with the other group. However, when the culture of the socially superior group is not well adapted to environmental conditions, its members may do the bulk of the borrowing. What happens when a group of fighting nomads conquers and settles among a civilized urban people would be a case in point. This situation has occurred repeatedly in the Old World and has always resulted in the originally nomadic aristocracy taking over most of the culture conquered, reserving only those elements of their own culture which had become symbols of status. When the socially superior group also has the culture which is best adapted to the local conditions, the one-sidedness of the borrowing reaches a maximum. . . .

In most cases of fusion the culture exchange has not been so one-sided or the resulting culture so readily traceable to a single source. Due to the modification of borrowed elements and the adjustment of other parts of each culture to them, the end product of culture fusion resembles a chemical rather than a mechanical mixture. The resulting culture will not be a simple aggregation of elements all of which can be traced to one or the other of the parent cultures, but a new thing many of whose patterns cannot be directly referred to either. . . .

Where there is a strong desire on the part of members of an inferior group to become fused with those of a superior one, this individual-by-individual transfer is, in itself, a factor which accelerates the process of absorption. The more energetic and able members of the inferior group, those who might become leaders in its separate life, devote their efforts not to attaining status within it but to getting out of it. The fact that repudiation of the inferior group's culture becomes a technique for the achievement of individual success changes the attitude of the whole group toward it and hastens its elimination. . . .

It was pointed out . . . that factors of racial difference appear to be of little importance relative to the normal processes of culture transfer. However, they become of great importance in connection with fusion. If we consider this as a biological phenomenon race is still unimportant. Any two groups can hybridize successfully and we know that such mixture takes place whenever two groups are brought into contact. Even the most elaborate social regulations have never been able to prevent this. The importance of race in fusion situations lies in the fact that obvious physical differences between groups can be used as criteria for the assignment of social status. Most contact situations entail attitudes of superiority and inferiority between the groups involved. Even in the absence of practical advantages from membership in the superior group there are prestige advantages which its members rarely desire to share. The desire of members of the inferior group to get into the superior one is usually met by an equally strong desire on the part of those already there to keep them out. As long as the differences between the two groups are purely cultural this presents practical difficulties. Members of the inferior group cannot be distinguished from members of the superior one once they have assumed its language and habits. The ease with which, here in the United States, persons of north European ancestry can transfer from immigrant to American society is a case in point. . . .

Where there are well-marked differences in physical type between the superior and inferior groups, it becomes easy to exclude members of the inferior group from the superior society. In spite of differences in the theoretical attitudes of various European groups toward natives, the color line is a fact in most contact situations. Easily recognizable racial differences delay fusion although it is highly questionable whether they are, in themselves, sufficient to prevent it. If the inferior group desires to be absorbed and holds to its wish, it probably is impossible to prevent fusion from taking place sooner or later. Even if the women of the superior group repulse all advances from men of the inferior one, a situation commoner in theory than in practice, the men of the superior group will rarely abstain from taking willing concubines. There is thus a steady transfer of blood from one group to the other with a consequent blurring of the original racial lines. When the two groups can no longer be distinguished physically, no amount of artificial regulation can prevent their social fusion.

Fusion may be either a slow or a rapid process, but it seems to be the ultimate outcome of any contact situation in which one or both groups wish to fuse. As we have already seen, there may be situations in which this attitude is not present. Both of the groups involved may be convinced of their own superiority so that the resistance to fusion is mutual and therefore more than doubly effective. Under such conditions the offspring of mixed unions will be looked down upon by both and, instead of bringing the groups closer together, will form a new caste at the bottom of the social order. . . .

There may also be changes in the attitudes of both groups toward fusion at different points in the contact continuum. Social lines may be drawn more or less rigidly as time goes on. Thus the eighteenth-century Europeans seem to have been more receptive to elements of Oriental culture and more willing to accord social equality to members of Oriental groups than their descendants are today. . . .

There is one series of attitude changes which has repeated itself in so many contact situations that it might be said to constitute a recognizable pattern. This series begins with attitudes of respect and admiration on the part of the dominated group, coupled with a sincere desire to acquire the culture of the dominant one and an expectation of finally being fused with it. . . . Critical and hostile attitudes are rarely assumed by any large proportion of the inferior group as long as fusion is recognizably in progress. If the members of the inferior group know that there is a genuine possibility for the ultimate removal of their social disabilities, they will put up with all sorts of hardships and even injustices, considering them transitory phenomena. . . . It is only with the loss of the hope of fusion, which presents itself to the individual in terms of full social acceptance and equal opportunity, that the difficulties imposed upon the inferior group by the contact situation come strongly to the fore.

Such states of disappointment and of disillusionment with the new order may very well be the starting points for nativistic movements. We have defined such movements as a glorification of past or passing phases of culture with a conscious attempt to re-establish them. Nativistic movements are thus characterized by two sets of phenomena which really are of different orders. The glorification of past or passing phases of culture is an almost universal accompaniment of situation of culture change. It is in no way related to culture contact per se. Even in the most progressive and forward-looking community, changes in culture produce some individual discomforts. At least some members of the group will develop nostalgic attitudes toward a past which appears rosy in the light of present difficulties. The more intense and widespread the discomfort due to change, the more widespread these attitudes are likely to be. When culture change is complicated by the presence of another group and by feelings of inferiority toward it, glorification of the old culture provides a convenient compensatory mechanism. A society which can find nothing to plume itself on in the present can bolster its self-respect by contemplating the real or imaginary glories of its past. It may even attempt to revive certain aspects of its past culture as a way of emphasizing these attitudes. Such revivals are rigidly circumscribed by the nature of the existing culture. They are never of a far-reaching sort and they do not have to be. A revival of native literature or peasant art is as effective as a symbol and a reminder of the past as a reversion to an earlier economic system would be and at the same time vastly more convenient. . . .

Violent and explosive nativistic movements seem to require a special combination of circumstances—subjection to another group, economic hardship, and loss of hope of bettering conditions by practical means. Apparently no one of these conditions is enough to produce such movements in the absence of the others nor does the whole series always produce them.

All the violent nativistic movements which have been studied include a large element of supernaturalism. How strong the stimuli have to be before such movements take shape is probably correlated to a considerable extent with the group's attitudes toward the supernatural and the strength of their belief in its ability to alter conditions in the material world. In such movements the revival of past phases of culture is not an end in itself but a magical technique. In other words, the group does not attempt to return to its earlier culture because it feels that culture to be superior under current conditions. It does so in the hope of enlisting supernatural aid to change the current conditions. At the basis of all such movements lies a quite irrational system of associations. Since the people were happy and contented in the old days when they had a particular culture in a particular environment, it is felt that a return to the culture will, in some way, re-establish the total original configuration. At the same time, it is significant that such movements always retain enough touch with reality not to imply a complete return to the earlier conditions. Those elements of the current culture which are obviously superior to their earlier equivalents will be miraculously preserved. Thus in the Ghost Dance the millennium was to leave the Indians still in possession of rifles and metal cooking pots and, in some versions, of the White men's houses and stock.

No group has ever attempted to revive its total culture as it existed at any given point in the past. The revivals are selective and constitute symbols which are manipulated to produce certain results. In violent nativistic movements this manipulation is along magical lines and is foredoomed to failure. In the quieter and more normal type of nativistic movement the manipulations rely for their effect upon psychological factors which are operative in all groups. As a result, such movements very often succeed not in their avowed purpose of revivifying a dead culture but in their actual purpose of bolstering the ego of the group in the face of conditions of inferiority.

In conclusion it may be said that the only constant phenomenon in situations of continuous first-hand contact, i.e., acculturation under our definition, is the establishment, in the two cultures involved, of mutual modifications and adaptations which will enable the two groups to live together. Even this is not absolutely constant, for one of the groups may not succeed in making such adaptations and become extinct in consequence. However, if both groups survive, the adaptations will be made. One of the most tragic features of our own dealings with the American Indians has been the constant changes in policy which, together with tribal removals, have rendered the adaptations which they successively developed successively unworkable. Lastly, everything indicates that the ultimate end of situations of close and continuous first-hand contact is the amalgamation of the societies and cultures involved, although this conclusion may be postponed almost indefinitely if there is opposition to it on both sides.

Whether acculturation offers a legitimate field for independent study the reader must judge for himself. At least it should have been made clear that the phenomena associated with culture change, culture transfer, and group contact are present here in their most complex form and with the largest possible number of variables operative. These phenomena are so poorly understood at present that there is such a lack of actual factual material by which conclusions can be checked that any statements made about them must be considered tentative and valid only in the light of our present very limited information. The most that can be said is that the conclusions which have been presented appear to check with the facts presented in the accompanying papers and also in other studies of contact situations.

"Problems of Status Personality" was presented at a Viking Fund interdisciplinary conference, Culture and Personality, which was published by S. Stansfeld Sargent and Mariam W. Smith in 1949. Though brief, it represents Linton's fundamental points of

agreement and disagreement with Abram Kardiner. While Kardiner stresses such "basic institutions" as childhood training practices, Linton stresses structural factors such as the necessity of conformity to status-roles.

Problems of Status Personality

✤ In discussing the concept of Status Personality and the problems connected with its study, I believe that we can take as our basic postulate that the members of different societies show different personality norms. Various investigators have coined various terms to designate these norms: "National (or Tribal) Character," "Modal Personality," "Basic Personality Type," and so forth. While there may have been slight differences in the meanings of these terms when they were coined, they seem to be used interchangeably at present. Since the word "Character" has an established meaning which does not seem appropriate to the phenomenon in question, I prefer to ignore the first of these designations. "Modal Personality" and "Basic Personality Type" seem to differ mainly in stressing different aspects of the same phenomenon, as will be pointed out shortly. Actually, the choice of terms is of no great importance as long as we have a clear understanding of what we are talking about.

The "Modal Personality" for any society can be established directly and objectively by studying the frequencies of various personality configurations among a society's members. The fact that, to the best of my knowledge, it never has been so established does not invalidate the concept. My own experience, based on informal observation rather than exact tests, suggests that, given a sufficiently large sample, any personality configuration found in one society can be matched in other societies. However, there can be no question that frequencies of various personality configurations do differ markedly from one society to another. A configuration which must be considered normal for one society on purely statistical grounds may be highly aberrant for another. The Modal Personality for any society corresponds to this statistically established norm.

The term "Basic Personality" or "Basic Personality Type" reflects a dynamic approach to this phenomenon of Modal Personality. Numerous investigations have made it clear that the Modal Personality for any society bears a close relation to the culture of that society. To put the matter in its simplest terms, the sort of people who are most numerous in any society are also the sort of people who would find its culture congenial in any case. They are the sort of people who, if they had come into the society from the outside, with their personalities already formed, would have found it easy and pleasant to learn the society's ways, to accept its values and attitudes, and to become respected citizens.

This congruity between the Modal Personality and the culture of various societies seems to be quite as characteristic for groups of mixed racial ancestry as for those which are relatively pure. We may assume from this that the culture of any society plays a dominant role in shaping the personalities of most of the society's members. That there are other than cultural factors involved is indicated by the appearance of aberrant personalities in all societies. However, we still know so little of just what these factors may be that it seems best to ignore them for the present. We will limit our discussion to the interrelations of the "normal" members of a society with their culture.

The relation between "normal" individuals and the culture of their society is unquestionably a reciprocal one. It is a "feed back" phenomenon of the sort which is just now attracting the attention of workers in many other branches of science. On the one hand, the culture shapes the personalities of a society's members. On the other, the members of a society are responsible, in the long run, for shaping the society's culture. The processes involved are complicated but quite recognizable.

Societies and their associated cultures are continuums. The individuals who enter such a continuum, usually by the accident of birth, are exposed to cultural influences during the entire time they remain within it. These influences are represented concretely by what other members of the society say and do and, especially during the early part of the individual's sojourn, by what they say and do to him. Because of his complete dependence on others, the infant or small child is particularly susceptible to cultural conditioning. The findings of clinical psychology seem to indicate that most of the basic patterns present in the adult personality are established during the first few years of life. Moreover, a series of studies carried out on various non-European societies has demonstrated the existence of certain fairly constant linkages between particular techniques of child care and particular features of the Modal Personalities of these societies.

As the individual grows up, his relation to his society's culture gradually changes. When the basic patterns of his personality have become established, cultural pressures seem to operate mainly to reinforce the results of his early experience. How far such pressures may be able to alter the basic patterns is a question which we cannot settle at present. As we shall see, the systematic study of Status Personalities may throw more light on this problem than any other line of research can. However, it is safe to say that the maximum influence of culture upon personality is exerted during the individual's childhood.

In contrast to this, the individual's potentialities for influencing culture are negligible in childhood and reach maximum intensity when he is an adult. His influence may be exerted in either of two ways: (1) He may function as an active agent in culture change, operating either as an inventor or as an innovator for borrowings from other cultures. Such activities seem to be confined to small numbers of individuals in any society; (2) he may function as a more or less passive agent in culture change through his ability to accept or reject the new items introduced to the society by the inventor or innovator. Most of the members of any society maintain this role and its importance must not be underestimated. Unless a substantial number of a society's members finds a new idea or form of behavior congenial, the new thing has no chance of becoming a part of the society's culture. Even established culture patterns are liable to elimination or modification when they cease to be congenial.

All the evidence now available indicates that cultures are constantly changing although the rate of change may vary not only from one culture to another but also at different points in the same culture continuum. Human societies normally persist for many generations and are composed, at any given time, of individuals at all age levels.

It follows that all types of interaction between the culture of a society and the individuals who compose it are going on simultaneously. At the very moment when the culture is shaping the personalities of young individuals and reinforcing many of the personality characteristics of their elders it is also being shaped through the activities of inventors, innovators, or simple selectors.

The personality characteristics which are "normal" (in the sense of "most frequent") for the members of a society at any time will exert a strong influence on current developments within its culture. It is the organized aggregate of these characteristics which has been referred to as the "Modal Personality" or "Basic Personality" for a society. Since this configuration seems to be basic to much of culture change and to underlie most, if not all, of the variations in personality which any society recognizes and approves, "Basic Personality" seems to be the more appropriate term for it when dynamics are involved.

The members of any society are usually unconscious of their own Basic Personality, dismissing its characteristics as those of human nature in general. However, they are if anything overconscious of certain variations in personality which their society not only permits but also encourages. Thus all societies assume that the individuals who occupy certain positions in their sytsems of organization will, as a group, show personality norms differing from those of individuals in certain other positions. All societies seem to assume this for such groups as men and women or chiefs and commoners while many of them extend the concept to include practitioners of certain trades. Thus less than a century ago, North Europeans assumed that all tailors were cowardly, all butchers brutal if not sadistic, and all blacksmiths men of strong character.

The study of such Status Personalities, as I have chosen to call them, can scarcely fail to produce results which will be significant for the understanding of many personality phenomena. Common status provides one of the simplest and at the same time most significant frames of reference within which groups of individuals can be observed and compared. Persons who share a common status within a society are all subject to the same sort of formal social pressures and are expected to learn and adhere to similar culturally patterned forms of overt behavior. A comparative study of how different individuals within such a group react to these common pressures and of the personality factors underlying their reactions should prove exceedingly enlightening.

Social positions, i.e., statuses, are of various sorts and each sort carries its own potentialities for personality study. Those supposedly linked with differing personality norms fall at once into two classes: (1) Those which derive from a class or caste structure within the society and (2) Those which do not involve factors of class or caste. Any society with a fully developed class structure is really an organized aggregate of subsocieties each with its own subculture. The class-linked status personalities in such a society correspond more closely to Basic Personalities in both genesis and characteristics than they do to the status personalities of the second type. In simple terms, the members of each class are shaped by their own culture and their personality norms derive first of all from this culture and only secondarily from the culture of the larger configuration of which their class forms a part.

The study of class-linked status personalities within a single society should throw considerable light on the dynamics of personality formation and especially on the relations between patterns of early childhood care and adult personality. One might anticipate that methods of child care would vary from class to class, but it seems that this is by no means always the case. Thus in many class-organized non-European societies the patterns of infant care seem to be closely similar throughout. Even in societies where the ideal techniques of child rearing are different for different classes, the actual techniques may be very similar. There seems to be a universal tendency for upper class parents to leave the care of their children, especially infants, to lower class servants. This is easily understandable in view of the oppressiveness of the infants' physical demands. Such servants, unless kept under constant surveillance, will deal with their charges according to the culture patterns of their own class.

During the last few years, a number of investigators have attempted to account for the observed differences of Basic Personality in various societies on the basis of the differing infantile experience of persons raised in these societies. Great stress has been placed on the experience derived from patterns of nursing, swaddling, sphincter control, etc. It would seem that a crucial test of these theories could be made by comparing status groups who had received the same treatment in these respects while being required by class differences to adjust to widely different adult roles.

Among the status personalities which are not class linked, two types seem to be of particular interest for dynamic studies. One of these consists of those statuses whose demands upon the individual are consistent throughout most of the life cycle. An example of this would be the assignment of different personality norms to men and to women. All societies have different personality stereotypes for the two sexes although, as Dr. Margaret Mead has delighted in pointing out, the content of these stereotypes may vary considerably from one society to another. A second example would be the assignment of a distinct status personality to eldest sons in certain societies which combine primogeniture with extended family leadership.

In both these cases the individual's adult role can be predicted from the moment of birth and steps can be taken to train him for it in terms of both techniques and value-attitude systems. As far as one can determine from simple observation, most societies have developed effective methods for doing this. While physiological differences may complicate the problem in the case of male and female status personalities, they would not enter into the other example cited. Eldest sons as a group would not differ significantly from any other sons, yet societies in which lack of aggression and fear of assuming leadership or accepting responsibility are the rule still contrive to instill these qualities into their potential family heads. It is significant to note that in neither of the cases just cited is there any recognizable difference in infantile care. Males and females, eldest and younger sons are subjected to identical patterns of nursing, swaddling, sphincter control, etc. The shaping of the individual for his or her adult role is undertaken deliberately and is delayed until after the dawn of intelligence.

Still more interesting than such life-long status personalities are those which are linked with certain periods in the individual's life cycle. There are numerous societies, including our own, in which the same individual is expected to manifest different personality characteristics at different age levels. Often he is expected to undergo a veritable psychological transformation when passing from one age group to the next, as from adolescent to adult status or from adult to old. Since our own society expects a transformation of personality between adolescence and maturity, we take it for granted that such a transformation can occur and try to account for it in terms of the changing physiology of this life period. We anticipate no change in personality between adult and aged statuses and I believe that most students of personality would doubt that any significant change could occur at this point.

In view of the foregoing, it is interesting to note that there is at least one society, the Comanche, whose patterns are diametrically opposed to our own in this respect. Comanche childhood is a careful and continuous preparation for full adult status. As soon as the child can walk he is dressed in a miniature replica of adult costume. He is given tasks which are like those of adults but carefully adjusted to his strength. Every device is employed to make him vigorous, individualistic, aggressive, and competitive in order that he may become a successful warrior. The behavior which his society expects of him is consistent throughout and even the arrival of puberty passes without ceremonial recognition. However, if he survives a life of warfare until he reaches the point where his physical powers begin to wane, his personality is expected to undergo a sudden and complete transformation. As an old man he is expected to be docile, cooperative, good to women and children, and willing to risk slights and offenses to his dignity by acting as mediator in quarrels between younger men. It would be interesting to know how many individuals were able to really experience such a personality transformation. Of the old men whom I knew several, after fair success in the warrior role, had sunk back into that of old men with considerable satisfaction. I gathered that they had become very bored with fire eating and honor watching and were glad to take a rest.

The first problem which confronts the investigator in any study of status personality is that of how far the overt behavior of individuals, when culturally patterned, can be used as an index of personality. It seems that given an adequate system of rewards and punishments, any individual can learn to perform any role at least insofar as the behavior expected of him is routine. Undoubtedly there are many individuals in all societies who find their social roles uncongenial; yet most of them contrive to function with moderate success and without too great psychological discomfort. They may even succeed in adjusting to two or three different roles, each of which would appear to be congruous with a different sort of personality, and in shifting from one to another of these according to the cues which they recognize. The petty official obsequious to superiors, a tyrant in the bosom of his family, and a model of good fellowship around election time would be a case in point.

Most "normal" individuals seem to have this chameleon ability fairly well developed. It appears to be weakest in certain types of neurotics and one wonders whether the slight attention paid to it by some Depth Psychologists, especially by certain Psychoanalysts, may not be related to the highly selected subjects on whom their theoretical formulations have been based. Here again the study of series of individuals within clearly defined status groups would be exceedingly informative.

As has already been said, all societies have developed conscious stereotypes for certain Status Personalities. Such stereotypes may or may not correspond to reality. Once firmly established, they themselves become culture patterns which may be transmitted verbally long after they have lost any justification which they may have originally had. An excellent case in point would be the stereotype for Negro as contrasted with White personality norms in our own society. Anyone who has come to know a number of present-day Negroes as individuals knows how far the carefree, good-natured, shiftless stereotype differs from the hostile and anxiety-ridden reality. Nevertheless, in dealing with Whites, the Negro will, with few exceptions, behave in the ways that the stereotype calls for since this is the behavior which is most immediately effective.

I am ready to go a step farther and suggest that until we have more information than is now available, we cannot dismiss the possibility that Status Personalities are really cultural fictions. It is quite conceivable that we may be dealing with differences in complicated and coherently organized roles rather than in personality norms. The stereotypes for Status Personalities which all societies have developed perform important functions. On the one hand, they reconcile the society as a whole to what might otherwise seem cruelty or injustice toward particular groups within it. If most of a society's members believe that such groups differ from themselves in aims and attitudes, they will not identify with them or suffer any pangs of conscience. On the other hand, Status Personality stereotypes may do much to reconcile a society to domination by small numbers of aristocrats who are represented as having all the qualities which the society idealizes.

Thanks to the use of Rorschach, Thematic Apperception, and an increasing battery of similar tests, the reality of different Basic Personality configurations for different societies seems to be firmly established. It remains now to apply such tests to different status groups within single societies. As far as I can discover, little or no work along these lines has been done to date. The Social Scientists who could delimit such status groups have lacked psychological interests while the Psychologists have lacked the techniques for delimiting such groups for themselves. It is to be hoped that the two disciplines can get together in the near future and pool their abilities.

"The Scope and Aims of Anthropology" is the first chapter of The Science of Man in the World Crisis, *edited by Linton (Columbia University Press, 1945) just as World War II came to a close. It illustrates well Linton's belief in the necessity of interdisciplinary research and in the usefulness of the social sciences in approaching broad social issues. Combined with* Most of the World, *which he edited in 1949 (Columbia University Press), this paper illustrates his conviction that anthropology should play an important role in international understanding and international relations.*

The Scope and Aims of Anthropology

✣ The present period is the first in the world's history in which men have turned to science for aid rather than to the supernatural.

Unfortunately those who seek such aid too often find themselves in the position of a sick man shifted from specialist to specialist without obtaining any over-all picture of his illness or any one plan for its cure. Science began as natural philosophy, a particular way of looking at the world with particular techniques for studying it. At its inception it had a universality comparable to that of the Church. However, no sooner had it won its right to live than it began to propagate itself by an amoeba-like process of fission. It ceased to be one science and became instead a series of sciences, each of which had its own interests and its own rigidly delimited subject matter. Even the amoeba has learned the advantage of occasional conjugations from which both parties emerge invigorated, but it seems that many scientists have still to learn it. During the last hundred years the tendency has been for each science to hold the others at a safe distance, browsing on its own selected pastures and learning more and more about less and less. Although this is undoubtedly due in part to the vast accumulation of factual knowledge which this period has seen, it also represents a definite attitude whose effects have been stultifying. It is true that no one scientist can possibly acquaint himself with the whole range of scientific knowledge as it exists today, yet it is quite possible for any man to know the conclusions which have been arrived at in several sciences other than his own and to apply these to his own problems. Most of these conclusions are relatively simple and the time would seem to be ripe for a new synthesis of science, especially of those sciences which deal with human beings and their problems.

By its very definition, the science of anthropology makes a bid for this position. In all English-speaking countries the term is taken to mean "the science of man and his works." In Europe the term has been given a somewhat different meaning, being limited to the study of man's physical characteristics, but we will adhere to the broader definition. Throughout its entire history, anthropology has differed from such familiar sciences as zoology or physiology or genetics in one important respect. Where these sciences have concentrated upon phenomena of certain limited sorts wherever they occurred in nature, anthropology has concentrated its interest upon a single organism, man, and has tried to understand all sorts of phenomena as they affected him. It has attempted to find out all that there was to be known about this curious biped and his still more curious behavior. This has not improved its standing among the sciences. Followers of the natural and physical sciences have tended to regard the anthropologist as an anachronism, the last survivor of that class of pleasant gentlemen who, in the eighteenth century, knew something about almost everything but not much about anything. However, it is equally possible to regard anthropology as the first of a series of synthesizing sciences, the need for which is becoming ever more apparent. The writer feels that it is to the credit rather than the discredit of anthropologists that most of them have been willing to employ the techniques and conclusions of other sciences and to follow problems wherever they led without paying much attention to scientific borders and "No Trespassing" signs.

Even with the best intentions, anthropology has not been able to avoid the atomistic tendencies which have characterized science in general. The field which anthropology has attempted to cover is so vast and involves phenomena of so many different sorts that no one individual can be intimately acquainted with the whole of it. It has, therefore, followed the familiar pattern of fission and split into a number of subsciences, each of which has developed its own group of specialists. It has even had its minor civil wars over the exact limits of such subsciences and their relative importance. However, the modern tendency is to pay less and less attention to these limits and to recognize that all these subsciences are parts of a whole, some useful for solving one problem and some useful for another, but all necessary to the understanding of human existence.

The sharpest split within anthropology has been that along the line laid down in the very definition of the science, the distinction between man and his works. The study of man as an animal, one of many mammalian species, leans almost exclusively upon the techniques and conclusions developed by the natural sciences. Actually, it can use only a small part of the techniques, since human beings do not take kindly to being made the subject of experiment. Again and again it has had to wait for the natural sciences to clear up some point by animal experiment. Thus the controlled breeding of human beings presents great difficulties even in a totalitarian state. The understanding of human heredity and the clearing up of various problems connected with the human varieties which we call races was impossible until the geneticists' work with fruit flies and rats had provided the necessary information. On the other hand, the study of human behavior can receive little help from the findings of natural science. Although some of the simplest behavioral phenomena, such as learning processes, can be studied in animals and by experimental techniques most of them have no close parallel at the animal level. This is especially true with respect to the complex phenomena involved in organized social life. Although in this field anthropologists have been able to use some of the techniques developed by the social sciences, they rarely had to wait upon the development of such techniques. In fact they have been able to contribute quite as much to the development of these sciences as they have received from them.

The two great divisions of anthropology which deal respectively with man and with his works are known as physical anthropology and cultural anthropology. This division dates back to the very beginnings of anthropology and each branch of the science has followed its own line of development and produced its own group of specialists. Very few individuals have been active in and familiar with both fields, with the result that the two have largely lost touch with each other. It seemed for a time that the separation might be a permanent one, with physical anthropology becoming completely aligned with the natural sciences and cultural anthropology with the social sciences. However, they are now beginning to be drawn together again as we become increasingly conscious of the influence of certain physiological factors upon culture and vice versa. This process is being reinforced by a sort of renaissance in the field of physical anthropology. After generations of preoccupation with bones, bodily measurements, and systems of racial classification, the physical anthropologists are beginning to turn to studies of a more dynamic sort and to recognize that in these cultural factors have to be taken into account.

Each of the main divisions of anthropology has undergone further differentiation. Physical anthropology has split into human paleontology and somatology; cultural anthropology into archeology, ethnology, and linguistics. The names of these subsciences are daunting, but the sciences themselves, or at least their more spectacular findings, will be familiar to most readers. Human paleontology deals with the origins and evolution of our species, especially as these are revealed by fossils. Every time one reads of the finding of another fragment of some ancient half-human form, with a discussion of its relations to modern man, he is coming into contact with this branch of anthropology. This is, or was before the present war, one of the most rapidly developing areas in the science. Every year brought forth new finds and new disputes as to where even the old ones belonged in the human family tree. What the investigators in this field have lacked in numbers they have more than compensated for in enthusiasm. The exceedingly fragmentary nature of the finds, and the fact that many of them were one of a kind, have simply given the human paleontologists more room for maneuver on the field of battle. The only undisputed facts which have emerged from this work so far are that there were a number of ancient species which were more or less intermediate between men and apes and that one or more of these must have been the ancestors of modern man. Which one has the proud distinction is still an unsettled question. Since even the final establishment of the "missing link" will not be of much aid to his descendants in their present difficulties, the results of this branch of anthropology have been excluded from the present symposium.

Somatology deals with modern man in all his physical aspects. The general characteristics of our species as vertebrates and mammals are well taken care of by such general sciences as anatomy and physiology. The somatologists have, therefore, concentrated upon the study of human varieties, their differences, and the probable causes of these differences. Until very recent times, most of their attention has been concentrated upon the classification of the various human varieties— that is, races—and their possible relationships. The classifications which they have developed still depend mainly upon simple, superficial characteristics such as skin color and hair form. In recent years attention has been turned to less obvious but intrinsically more important differences such as blood types, differences in musculature, and so on. Still more recently, somatologists have begun to study group differences in growth rates, time of sexual maturation, metabolic rates, and disease immunities. Here many of their findings may be of immediate practical value. The head shape of a particular human variety has little importance except in cases where it has been given social significance, but the adjustment of a particular variety to certain conditions of altitude and temperature, or its inherited resistance to malaria, may be of great importance for any resettlement program.

The whole concept of race, so vigorously misused in certain quarters, lies within the field of somatology, and we must look to it for the final settlement of those problems which are connected with race at the physiological as distinct from the social level. Unfortunately, such problems are in the minority. Aside from the demonstrable fact that certain races do better than others in certain environments, the main significance of racial differences in a modern world lies in the social values attached to them. Our present frictions arise not from anything inherent in racial differences but from the fact that such differences have come to be used as indicators of social status. The average individual in our own society is quite unable to say which of the various European racial types most of his friends belong to, since this is a matter of no social importance. At the same time he will be conscious of very small differences in physical type when these indicate that the individual belongs to some socially differentiated group such as the Jew or the Negro.

Turning to the field of cultural anthropology and its subsciences, we find that the subscience of linguistics is, at present, the most isolated and self-contained. The study of languages can be and largely has been carried on with little relation to other aspects of human activity. The great diversity of languages, especially among the so-called primitive peoples, and their curious and complex structures affords the investigator unlimited material for research. When presented with the results of such research the layman is likely to be reminded of Abe Martin's dictum: "It takes years to become a champeen checker player and what then?" However, the analysis and classification of languages, like the classification of human varieties, is only a first step. In language and its diversities the scientist has a tool which should ultimately prove of great value for understanding the deeper levels of both individual and group psychology. Although we are taught to regard language as primarily a means of communication, it is equally important as a tool for thinking. This is the area in which the wide range of existing linguistic forms is most significant. Any idea can be communicated in any language if the speaker will take time enough, but the concepts which are an integral part of all linguistic forms have a subtle influence upon the individual's ways of thinking. These concepts are even more compulsive because they are totally unconscious.

An example may help to make this clear. The lack of an inanimate gender in English gives an animistic slant to all our thinking. An inanimate gender is not to be confused with a neuter one. *It* in English can refer to inanimate objects, but it can also refer to animate ones such as ghosts or, at some risk of the parents' displeasure, babies. *He* and *She*, with their implicit ascription of sex, always imply animation. The result of this linguistic accident is that we cannot refer to anything, even the most abstract concept, without unconsciously endowing it with life and capacity for volition. We have to personify everything we talk or even think about. Those who try to work with abstractions find themselves in a constant battle with this tendency toward personification, and no matter how careful they are it slips through occasionally to interfere with their clarity of thought. If English had an inanimate gender, as many other languages do, the words used for abstractions would, in themselves, provide a constant corrective for such a tendency.

Finally, it should be noted that the study of linguistics is not to be confused with the trick of learning languages. Understanding of the structure of a language may be an aid in learning it but it is by no means necessary. Note the experience of children and of those who "pick up" a foreign language without any knowledge of its grammar. There are plenty of people who can speak several languages while remaining blissfully unconscious of the structure of any of them. That linguistics ultimately will be of great value for the understanding of human behavior and especially of human thought processes can hardly be doubted. However, work along these lines has barely begun and linguistics is still unable to make any great contribution toward the solution of our current problems. For that reason it has been ignored in the present volume.

The two other subsciences in the field of cultural anthropology, namely archeology and ethnology, bear somewhat the same relation to each other that human paleontology bears to somatology in the field of physical anthropology. Archeology deals with the beginnings of culture and with those cultures or phases of culture which are now extinct. Ethnology deals with the living cultures of mankind in all their variety. Archeology is, perhaps, the most popular branch of anthropology and the ones whose findings are best known to the average layman. The results of various "digs" are constantly noted in the newspapers so that, to cite a single case, the name of an obscure Egyptian king, Tut-ank-amen, has become almost a household word. In general, archeologists try to discover and interpret that part of our past which is not revealed by written records. The study of the recorded past is assigned to the field of history. Since men have been writing for, at most, 6,000 years while our species has been in existence for at least 100,000 years, the archeologist has plenty of room for his operations. Moreover, it is only under exceptional conditions that written records tell us much about the life of the common man in any society. Ancient scribes usually wrote for and about kings and priests. Even our knowledge of such a well-documented civilization as that of the Romans has been tremendously enlarged by such excavations as those at Pompeii.

For the archeologist himself this science provides a happy combination of the thrills of research with those of treasure hunting, plus the added advantage of salary and expenses. For the wealthy backer it provides tangible, visible returns for the money invested, plus a complete absence of anything which might disturb the social status quo. It is not surprising, therefore, that archeological studies are usually easy to finance and that the science has progressed by leaps and bounds. The war has brought some interruption, but in spite of this it seems probable that another fifty years will give us a fairly clear picture of man's past in most parts of the world. This applies, of course, to those aspects of the past which are reflected in imperishable objects. We can discover what sort of tools an ancient society used, what its members ate, what sort of houses they lived in, and how they disposed of their dead, but archeology cannot tell us whether they were addicted to wife beating.

Although the immediate and obvious purpose of archeological work is to fill out our factual knowledge of man's past, its ultimate purpose is to give us an understanding of the processes involved in the growth, flowering, and collapse of civilizations and the factors which may be responsible for these. This is also the ultimate aim of history, but in the absence of written records the archeologist has developed new techniques, borrowing from other sciences in the process. He can deduce the opening of new trade routes from the chemical analysis of fragments of metal or pottery and, with the aid of dendrochronology, date the sack of a city from a few bits of charred timber. Moreover, the vast periods with which he deals makes it possible for him to discern the working of trends and cycles which operate in terms of millennia. He can trace the effects of climatic change or soil exhaustion in a way impossible to the historian and map the path of civilization on a wider field. Although the specific findings of archeology are not dealt with in the present volume, its conclusions with regard to process have become part of the common knowledge of all anthropologists working with phenomena of culture change. As such they are reflected in several of the contributions.

Ethnology deals with the ways of life of societies which are still extant or, at most, so recently extinct that fairly complete records are available. Every society has its own way of life, called its "culture" by anthropologists. The concept of culture is one of the most important tools of the anthropological investigator. Since one of the papers in this symposium is devoted to it, we need not deal with it here. At the same time, culture is such a convenient label for designating the organized collection of habits, ideas, and attitudes shared by the members of any society that it is almost impossible for any anthropologist to discuss these without using it. The task of the ethnologist is to study and compare cultures which are still going concerns and, from this, to develop conclusions which will hold good for culture in general. As in any other scientific work, the first step is the collection of facts about these cultures, and the work of the ethnologist takes him into all sorts of out-of-the-way places and among all sorts of people. Until very recent times, ethnologists have limited their fact-finding activities to the so-called primitive peoples, those living outside the scope of the few rich and complex cultures which we call civilizations. The more isolated such groups and the more widely their cultures differed from our own, the greater has been the interest in them. The old-line ethnologist is in the seventh heaven if he can find a group which has never seen a white man before, and he views the current opening up of the far corners of the earth with all the alarm of any craftsman whose livelihood is threatened. Ethnologists of the younger generation are less worried by the march of events. The study of cultures widely different from our own has led to the development of techniques for fact-finding and, above all, of attitudes of detachment, which lose none of their value when they are applied to civilized societies and cultures in transition. It is more romantic to study the natives of a South Sea island than a community of Iowa farmers, but the same scientific methods can be used with both and both can yield significant results. As long as human beings continue to live in communities and to develop special ways of life to meet special conditions the ethnologist will not be threatened with technological unemployment.

It might be questioned why the ethnologist should try to work with "primitive" peoples at all. It would seem that the culture of some dwindling tribe of Australian aborigines or American Indians, doomed to certain extinction, could give us little information which would be of use to us in meeting our own urgent problems. Actually, the study of one such tribe is of little practical value, but the study of a series of tribes, with later comparisons and analyses, may be exceedingly valuable. The social sciences are, by the very nature of their materials, debarred from using the techniques of controlled experiment which are the main stock in trade of the physical and even the natural sciences. No one can put a human society in a laboratory and see how it responds to various stimuli. The only substitute is to study and record societies as we find them and the more diverse the conditions under which they can be observed, the better the opportunity for arriving at conclusions which will hold good for all societies everywhere.

The ultimate aims of the ethnologist are essentially the same as those of the sociologist, economist, and, in part, the historian. All four are trying to understand how societies and cultures operate and why and how cultures change. They are attempting to arrive at certain generalizations, "laws" in common parlance, which will make it possible to predict the course of events and ultimately to control it. The main difference between ethnology on the one hand and sociology and economics on the other is that the latter have carried on their investigations almost entirely within the narrow frame of reference provided by our own society and culture. They have thus taken for granted many factors which have been characteristic of our own way of life during the last two or three hundred years but which are not an invariable accompaniment of social living. This might be well enough for the prediction and control of events in our own society if we lived in a period when most elements in our culture could be counted on to persist over long periods with little change. However, generalizations based upon such a narrow frame of reference have little value when the conditions which they take for granted are changing rapidly. The rise of new culture patterns and the disappearance of old ones robs such generalizations of most of their significance. Thus it would be an exceedingly optimistic economist who would try to use the generalizations based on our own business cycles of the past fifty years to predict what would happen in a totalitarian state. To be of value under the current conditions of rapid and basic change, generalizations about cultural and social phenomena will have to be based on the comparison of a much wider range of societies than the established social sciences have so far attempted to deal with. Such generalizations will have to get back to the basic principles on which all societies and cultures operate; the common denominators of human existence.

In the search for such common denominators the ethnologist has certain initial advantages. The "primitive" societies which have been, until very recent times, the center of his interest are, for the most part, small and compact and their cultures both simpler and better integrated than our own. There are thus fewer variables to be dealt with and a better chance of ascertaining how such societies and cultures really work. It is a general rule of science that research should proceed, when possible, from the simple to the complex, and the ethnologist has been doing just this in his social and cultural investigations. He hopes and believes that his findings in the simpler societies will help us to understand the more complicated ones, including our own. Still another factor which has worked to his advantage is that the investigator of an alien society can approach his work with a measure of detachment quite impossible in dealing with his own. Although no human being can approach the study of his own species in the same completely inpersonal terms which he might apply to a study of ants, he can come closest to it when the society in question is completely different from that in which he was reared. After the initial shock of discovering that wives in a polygynous society are strongly in favor of the institution or that old people ask their children to kill them when their rheumatism gets too troublesome, the ethnologist soon develops the attitude summed up in the familiar phrase: "Well, some do and some don't." The attitude is fatal to any reforming ardor, but it is a great help in acquiring the sort of accurate information needed for comparative studies. A high moral purpose has its uses in many situations but not in scientific research.

The various subsciences just discussed represent the content of anthropology as a formal discipline and as it is embalmed in the course announcements of most universities. However, there are important developments under way in various areas marginal to this long-established nucleus. The most important of these, at least from the point of view of furthering the development of pure science, is the emergence of a new field of research dealing with the interrelations of personality and culture. Until very recent times, ethnologists have deliberately limited their investigations to the mass phenomena of society and culture. They have regarded the individual as a mere culture carrier, one of a series of identical and interchangeable units. They have not troubled to enquire how he became a culture carrier or why, under certain circumstances, he departed from this passive role and initiated culture change. However, as time has gone on and as a better understanding of cultural phenomena has been achieved, the importance of these problems has become increasingly apparent. Lacking any techniques of his own for dealing with the individual, the ethnologist has turned to the personality psychologist for aid.

Personality psychology has followed a somewhat similar course in its development. It concentrated upon the individual and at first, under the influence of the natural sciences, tried to explain all individual similarities and differences on a physiological basis. Although the importance of environment in personality formation soon became apparent, this was used, at first, simply to explain individual differences. Lacking familiarity with the concept of culture and of any culture other than that of Europeans, the psychologists overlooked the importance of those experiences common to all individuals reared in our own civilization. In fact they took these results so much for granted that they posited various universal instincts to account for them. The discovery that personality norms differed for different societies and cultures came as a shock and one which necessitated a basic reorganization of many of their concepts. Since most of the personality psychologists were not in a position to obtain firsthand data on societies other than their own, and since they had developed no techniques for recording or organizing cultural material, they have turned to the ethnologists for help.

The result of these convergent developments has been the emergence of a new area of concentration. It is too early to say whether the study of personality and culture will become a distinct subscience, but it certainly manifests a high degree of hybrid vigor. Although barely twenty years old, it has already exerted considerable influence upon both of the parent sciences. It is giving the psychologists a much better understanding of the principles underlying personality formation and especially of the wide range of forms which the personalities of "normal" individuals may assume. Conversely, it has drawn the attention of the ethnologist to the differences in basic personality type for various societies; something which he had previously recognized without attempting to deal with or explain. Through this it is pointing the way toward the solution of one of the most difficult problems with which the ethnologist has to deal. Since the very beginning of his research he has sought to discover why certain societies develop particular foci of interest, why they accept or reject various innovations when no factors of utility seem to be involved, and why various cultures manifest different but consistent trends in their development. These things have so far been ascribed to historic accident, a manifest begging of the question. With the recognition of the existence of basic personality types and an understanding of how they are produced, such "accidents" become comprehensible and even, in certain cases, predictable. The importance of this for the planning and direction of culture change cannot be overestimated.

Although cooperation of anthropology with psychology has been, perhaps, the most fertile in results, anthropology has also worked with other disciplines toward the solution of common problems. There has been a steady exchange of ideas and techniques between ethnology and sociology. Sociology, as the older and also the more philosophic science, has far surpassed ethnology in the number and elaboration of its concepts and theories. It has also developed statistical techniques to a point far beyond anything ordinarily known to the ethnologist. However, it has limited itself almost exclusively to the study of our own institutions, so that many of its conclusions have not been applicable to mankind as a whole or even to our own society under conditions of rapid change. Contact with ethnology has provided sociology with new research techniques which are proving of especial value in the study of the smaller modern communities. It has also greatly expanded sociology's frame of reference, with consequence changes in certain of its theoretical formulations. In fact, at the level of theory the two sciences are converging so rapidly that it seems probable that within a few years there will be no important differences.

Another significant field of collaboration is that of somatology, physiology, and ethnology in the study of diet. This work, which has been carried on primarily under the direction of Dr. Margaret Mead and the sponsorship of the National Research Council, has been directed toward practical rather than theoretical ends. Its purpose has been to provide information on the basis of which nutritional standards in the United States might be improved and the feeding of foreign populations during the immediate post-war period carried out more effectively. The main contribution of ethnology in this work has been the recognition that food habits may be almost as important as food supply in determining whether a particular group is adequately nourished. However, such studies would seem to have important implications in connection with the possible physiological adjustment of various human groups to various diets, a field in which research has barely begun.

In addition to these cooperative activities in connection with adjoining sciences, anthropology has, in recent years, begun to invade the field of applied science. Its first excursions in this direction were, quite understandably, in connection with colonial administration. The more progressive colonial powers, notably England and Holland, learned by painful experience that an understanding of native institutions is a prerequisite for successful colonial government. They also discovered that it took years for the average individual to acquire such an understanding and that he was likely to make costly mistakes in the meanwhile. The trained ethnologist, on the other hand, could ascertain the nature of native institutions rapidly and accurately and pass on this knowledge in concise, usable form. Before the present war the use of ethnologists as colonial advisers was increasing rapidly. Under the progressive leadership of Commissioner John Collier they have even been introduced into our own Indian service. However, with few exceptions, such specialists have been used to devise ways and means for implementing policies rather than in the development of policies. The contributions which they have been able to make to the well-being of subject peoples has thus depended largely upon the intentions of their superiors. The very knowledge which makes it possible to control a native people with a minimum of friction can become a deadly weapon in the hands of those who wish to destroy a native society or to break down its culture for their own selfish ends.

More recently, a number of individuals who have been trained in ethnological theories and techniques have begun to employ these in the study of industrial relations, race relations, and the work of various social agencies. It is still too early to predict what the final outcome

173

of this work will be. The main contribution to date seems to have been that of bringing to such studies improved methods for the diagnosis of the social situations involved.

Although most of the current applications of anthropology use the data and techniques of ethnology, somatology also has numerous practical possibilities. To cite only a few of these, one anthropologist, Dr. M. R. Stein, has made an extensive study of racial differences in teeth and in the size and shape of the dental arch. On the basis of these studies an American firm has developed special dentures designed to meet the needs of various populations and these have proved highly profitable. An upper plate with jet black teeth, made for the Thailand trade, is one of the writer's treasured possessions. Somatologists can provide data on local and racial differences in size and body build which will be exceedingly useful to firms competing for foreign markets. They have also been employed during the present war in connection with the designing of better airplane cockpits and seats for paratroops, and they may well play their part in the post-war development of new furniture designs.

Such contributions are after all of minor importance, contributing to comfort rather than survival. Much more important is the knowledge which anthropologists are obtaining of the differing disease resistances of different human groups and the conditions of temperature, humidity, and altitude which are optimum for them. In the extensive movements of populations which will probably follow the war, this material should be taken into account. Thus it is an established fact that West African Negroes have a high tolerance for malignant malaria and are, with few exceptions, carriers of this disease. Racial groups who lack such immunity cannot be settled successfully in West Africa. Conversely, the introduction of West Africans into regions where there are suitable vectors for the disease but where it has not existed previously will cause great injury to the local populations. Many other examples of this sort could be cited.

This survey of the various areas of research and applied science in which anthropologists are at work should suffice to give some idea of the scope of formal anthropology. It naturally raises the question of where the limits of this science should be placed, but it seems to the

writer that this is largely an academic one. Every science can contribute to the development of several others and receive corresponding
aid from them. The present lines between disciplines are rarely inherent in the phenomena with which they have elected to deal and, as
time goes on, such lines seem to be maintained more by inertia and by
the vested interests of university departments than by anything else.
Anthropology is by no means the only discipline which has concerned
itself with the study of man. Sociology, economics, history, psychology, and even the newer geography are all primarily concerned with
him. Anthropology has differed from these mainly in the wider scope
of its interests and in its greater willingness to borrow and integrate
data from any source. The increasing cooperation between anthropologists and workers in other disciplines has filled some of the older
anthropologists with fears that their science may cease to exist as a
distinct discipline. They believe that if the present trends continue it
may be torn limb from limb and the bleeding fragments distributed
among its older and stronger neighbors. The writer believes such fears
to be groundless. It seems much more probable that it will become
the nucleus of a new Science of Man which will be broad enough in
its scope to include all aspects of human existence, civilized as well as
primitive. While there will always be need for specialists the crying
need of the present is for a synthesis of the knowledge which such
specialists have been able to accumulate.

Actually, such a generalized Science of Man is already taking shape
through the cooperation of members of the various specialized disciplines. The aim of this science is the same as that of all sciences. It
seeks to ascertain the processes and continuities involved in the phenomena with which it deals with a view to the prediction of events
and ultimately to their control. The phenomena of human existence
and especially of human behavior are exceedingly complex and the
work of reducing them to intelligible order has only begun. Anthropologists of the past generation, dazed by the variety of the cultures
with which they were becoming acquainted, doubted the possibility
of arriving at valid generalizations with respect to them. It must be
admitted at once that it is almost impossible to make any generalizations about the behavior of human beings in groups, that is, social

and cultural phenomena, to which there will not be a few apparent exceptions. However, this does not mean that such phenomena are without order. Every generalization must begin with the assumption of a particular frame of reference; a set of conditions under which it will hold good. Thus, to cite a familiar example, the law of falling bodies as it is stated in elementary physics books begins with the assumption that the bodies are falling in a vacuum, a condition never encountered in real life. The conditions under which societies and cultures have to operate are exceedingly complex and involve a great number of variable factors. In spite of this it is possible to arrive at a considerable number of generalizations which hold good for nearly all the cases which have been observed. Such generalizations can be made both with respect to the normal coexistence and functional interrelations of particular phenomena and with respect to various processes. Although they lack the absolute quality associated in our thinking with the term "law" and embody a lower factor of probability than do the laws of the physical or natural sciences, such generalizations are still valuable guides to the prediction of events. They will become even more so as the frames of reference within which they may be expected to hold good are more clearly delimited.

All the sciences which deal with man have developed a considerable number of such generalizations and have proved the worth of these by simple, pragmatic tests. Even when the generalizations have not been formally stated, they are implicit in the techniques and conceptual systems of such sciences. The principal task of the emergent Science of Man will be to draw these generalizations together and to develop new ones of wider scope and greater accuracy. Since this unification has barely begun, we must still turn to each of the specialized sciences concerned for its particular contributions—and each of them can contribute toward the solution of our current problems. It is for this reason that no attempt has been made to confine the contributions included in the present volume to the field of formal anthropology or the contributors to those who would call themselves anthropologists. It is enough that they are all co-workers in the Science of Man, attempting in one way or another to understand him and the phenomena which affect him and to find solutions for his problems.

" 'Primitive' Art" was published as the Preface to The Sculpture of Africa *by Eliot Elisofon (Frederick A. Praeger, Publishers, 1958), a lovely book of photographs of African wood carving. The essay appeared posthumously but it gives a clear picture of a subject which interested Linton throughout his life but which became more important to him in his later years.*

"Primitive" Art

❖ The term "primitive art" has come to be used with at least three distinct meanings. First and most legitimate is its use with reference to the early stages in the development of a particular art, as when one speaks of the Italian primitives. Second is its use to designate modern works of art executed by persons who have not had formal training in our own art techniques and aesthetic canons. Third is its application to the art works of all but a small group of societies which we have chosen to call civilized. The present discussion will deal only with the last.

The use of the term "primitive" to designate most of the world's cultures is an unfortunate aftermath of the ethnocentrism of the nineteenth-century European scientists who laid the foundations of modern anthropology. Elated by the success of the newly enunciated doctrines of biological evolution, they tried to apply these to the development of culture and saw all the simpler cultures as living fossils, surviving stages in a unilinear development of which European culture of the nineteenth century was the climax. This idea has long since been abandoned by anthropologists but, as so often happens with discarded scientific doctrines, it has become a part of the general body of popular misinformation. It still tinges a great deal of the popular thought and writing about the lives of non-European peoples.

Actually, there is no culture extant today which can be regarded as primitive. There are cultures of greater or less complexity and cultures which have a greater or smaller number of features in common with our own, but none of them are ancestral to the high cultures which we call civilizations. The way of life of an American Indian tribe or a group of Polynesian islanders does not represent a stage through which our own ancestors passed any more than a modern dog represents a stage in the evolution of the elephant. Every existing culture has had its own more or less independent evolutionary history.

The use of the term "primitive" with respect to the art styles developed by various societies is particularly deceptive. All existing art styles are results of long development and even those which appear simplest and least organized usually reveal a surprising degree of complexity and sophistication when one tries to reproduce them. Even the much-advertised animal art of the European cave man of twenty thousand years ago shows a high degree of conventionalization and a skill in abstraction comparable to that of the modern Japanese drawings in which the essential qualities of an animal are caught in half a dozen lines.

To call the uncivilized artist "primitive" is an even worse abuse of the term. Nothing could be more fallacious than to regard him as a retarded individual whose work can be considered on a par with that of a civilized child. He is an adult and often an exceedingly intelligent one. He possesses laboriously acquired skills, extensive technical knowledge, and clearly defined aesthetic standards. His work is never a simple, spontaneous outpouring of his desire for beauty. It is, in most cases, controlled by conventions considerably more rigid than those of our own art. If his work sometimes appears naive, it is because of the interests and values which these conventions reflect. If, in his representations, he ignores certain details of his subject, it is because to his society these details are either unimportant or taboo. Our own Victorian art treated certain details of human anatomy with a reticence incomprehensible to an African or Melanesian. To blame the primitive artist for such omissions is quite on a par with blaming a modernistic painter for not showing the individual leaves on a tree or the weave of the cloth in a subject's coat.

The similarities which have been pointed out between selected examples of "primitive" art and the work of children in our own society are purely fortuitous and depend upon a very careful selection of examples from both sources. No European child reared in a normal home with its books and pictures can be considered uninfluenced by European artistic conventions. Consciously or otherwise, he adheres to these conventions in his own work, and his "primitivity" is mainly a result of his lack of technical skill. No child, civilized or otherwise, ever produced anything remotely resembling the intricate grotesques of the New Zealand Maori or the abstract sculpture of West Africa. To find parallels for the first within our own art tradition one must go to the Gothic in its most virile period. The second finds a feeble reflection in the work of some of our modern sculptors working under the influence of African models which they have seen but rarely understood.

Objections of a different sort must be urged against the various attempts which have been made to equate the work of uncivilized artists with that of the insane in our own culture. The psychotic, like the child, has been strongly influenced by European art conventions but, unlike the child, he often has considerable skill and technical knowledge. The main difference between his work and that of the sane European artist is to be found in his bizarre associations of ideas and his use of purely personal symbolism. A particular schizophrenic may develop a configuration of interrelated ideas and symbols which resembles a culturally recognized configuration in some non-European society. If the insane European artist is skillful enough, his product may resemble that of the non-European one. However, this does not indicate that the non-European is psychotic or even indulging in the prelogical sort of thinking attributed to "primitives" by one school of social scientists. Every culture has developed configurations of associated ideas and symbols which appear illogical to an outsider. Our own association of lambs, doves, and crosses with a death cult, revealed in every cemetery, would look like the purest schizophrenia to an Eskimo.

Actually, the artists themselves provide the nearest thing to a common denominator of primitive and civilized art. That such artists are of different races means very little. In spite of long and eager search, no scientist has been able to demonstrate the existence of innate psychological differences in persons of different racial groups. An individual of any race reared as a member of a particular society will acquire the culture of that society. The differences between individuals are much more to the point. The primitive artist, like the civilized one, may be a genius, a clever and industrious mediocrity, or a mere copyist. Even if he is a genius, he will have his good and bad days, his successes and failures. Masterpieces are as rare in the art of uncivilized societies as they are in our own and as difficult for their creators to predict. There is plenty of bad primitive art, just as there is much bad civilized art, and the indiscriminate admiration of African or Oceanic sculpture simply because it is different certainly does not aid the cause of art or the development of a universally valid aesthetic.

The primitive artist's motives for being an artist are quite as diverse as those of his civilized counterpart. He may work because of an inner drive towards the creation of beauty, for profit, for prestige, or simply because it is part of his social role. There are many primitive societies in which all men of a particular class are expected to paint or carve or dance, much as all Victorian ladies were expected to do embroidery or paint in watercolors. The making of certain classes of art objects may also be a hereditary occupation vested in particular families or kin groups. Persons who thus have the artist's role thrust upon them are helped to acquire the skills needed to make them competent copyists, but there is plenty of evidence that the primitive genius, like the civilized one, is born and not made.

For reasons which will be discussed later, the members of a primitive community are in an excellent position to recognize superior artistic ability and quite ready to reward it. The finest examples of primitive art are, with few exceptions, the work of professionals. Although such work is rarely a full-time activity, the artist augments his regular income by taking commissions and adjusts his product to the demands of the market. The artist who is too radical soon finds himself without patrons. Far from being a free spirit, the primitive artist is subject to much the same pressures as his civilized counterpart.

It is exceedingly difficult to generalize about the primitive artist's attitude towards his work. The cultures grouped under the primitive heading are much too diverse. In all of them the individual tends to be more involved with the supernatural than the average member of our own society, but the extent to which this influences the artist's attitudes and working methods will vary not only from society to society but also from person to person. When the artist is a devout animist his relations with his tools and materials take on a mystic quality quite foreign to our own tradition. If he thinks of these as animate, intelligent beings he must also regard them as collaborators in the work of artistic creation. The rituals by which their willing cooperation is assured then become as important for the success of his work as any of his manual skills. Moreover, to the animist his own artistic product has a life of its own and a place in the universe, and part of his task is to arrange for these. Thus, the Iroquois mask maker carved his mask from the trunk of a living tree so that the tree's vitality would be transferred to it.

The highest development of this animistic attitude was in Polynesia. Here a single term, Tahunga, was used for both priest and master craftsman and, because of the intricacy of the ceremonial observances surrounding important work, the early writers on the region regarded the craftsman as a priest. Actually, it would be more accurate to regard the priest as a craftsman, one who worked with spirits and mana (impersonal supernatural power) as craftsmen of other sorts worked with more tangible materials. Among the Polynesian Marquesans the maker of images accompanied his work by reciting those parts of the Chant of Creation which gave the genealogies of the tools and materials he was using. His act of artistic creation was equated with procreation, and while the work was in progress his procreative powers were protected and strengthened by a strict taboo on copulation. As a final act, after the object was carved, he recited his own genealogy and his finished product stood forth as an independent Being, offspring of the artist and his materials and united with everything else in the universe by ties of kinship. Practices of this sort represent a rare and extreme development of animistic tendencies due to the Polynesian preoccupation with kinship and descent. However, the work of the artist, strictly predictable, tends to be hedged about by rituals and taboos designed to shield it from evil influences and insure its completion. Many of these rituals provide excellent examples of the interweaving of magical and practical elements which characterizes so many "primitive" activities. The spells to be recited are not infrequently work formulae, keeping in mind the various things which have to be done and the order in which they must be done to get the best results.

In spite of such involvements, the role of magic in primitive art should not be exaggerated. By no means all primitive art serves magical or religious purposes. There are usually nonrepresentational designs which are used simply for their aesthetic effect, while in groups in which sculpture or paintings are well developed these are often applied to utilitarian objects with no purpose other than their beautification. Even when magical considerations do enter into primitive art they are inextricably interwoven with aesthetic considerations, and it is often hard to tell which is dominant. Perhaps the only valid test is that of the extent to which the artist has elaborated and improved his design over and above the minimal magical requirements. The situation is, after all, very much like that which one encounters in European sacred art. A Renaissance Madonna was painted for a religious purpose and according to certain conventions which this purpose imposed, but these requirements could have been met by the crudest daub. Quite different motives lay behind its maker's desire for perfection in color and line. Similarly, a design carved on an arrow to give it magical power will often be amplified and elaborated to satisfy the "primitive" craftsman's desire for beauty. Man's search for supernatural aid and his search for beauty have always gone hand in hand.

It is only in those elaborate and self-conscious cultures which we call civilizations that this search for beauty has been intellectualized and made fully conscious. It seems probable that there are, at the foundation of all successful works of art, certain universally valid principles of harmony in form, color, and composition, but our difficulty in defining these is in itself proof of how little they have to do with the intellect. Neither artistic creation nor appreciation requires the intervention of verbal symbols, and to try to describe these processes is very much like trying to describe what goes on in one's own subconscious. Primitive artists are, almost without exception, unable to say why they have made a particular design or why they find one composition more satisfying than another. Many of our own best and most productive artists seem to be equally incoherent about these matters, and one suspects that the main difference between primitive and civilized at this point is that the primitive has never felt the need for rationalization after the fact, which has been responsible for our own intellectual involvement with aesthetic problems.

Since we can have no direct access to what goes on in the mind of the primitive artist, the only safe approach to his work is an objective one. The expression of his aesthetic urge is limited and directed by such factors as his techniques and materials, the artistic conventions preferred by his society, the beliefs and values which he shares with it, and the conditions under which he has to work. These things are usually ascertainable, and it is against the background which they provide that the artist's work must be studied and evaluated. The factors which are common to all primitive, in contradistinction to civilized, arts are not aesthetic ones. They derive from certain similarities in the technical problems with which all primitive artists are confronted and in the social and cultural milieus within which they have to function.

The primitive artist is normally a member of a small, closely knit community. Under ordinary circumstances even the professional works primarily for his neighbors and is strongly influenced by their opinion. Since he is personally known to his audience, it is quite unnecessary for him to sign his work, in the sense of placing any distinguishing mark upon it. The minor differences in style which emerge in even the most rigidly conventionalized art and the traces of his working methods are sufficient identification. In a few places, especially Africa, the primitive community may form part of a much larger social unit, but even so its members have few outside contacts. They are not completely cut off from the rest of the world, but new ideas reach them infrequently and are regarded with the suspicion which characterizes peasant communities everywhere. Minor variations on recognized themes are approved and good work is applauded, but radical innovations are discouraged.

This situation is not unlike that in European peasant communities prior to the modern technological revolution. However, primitive art differs from peasant art in certain respects. Peasant art fills a subsidiary niche in a larger artistic configuration. The peasant artist, even when semiprofessional, is keenly conscious of the existence of the fine arts and of their makers. He has a feeling of inferiority and regards his work as common art for common things. Moreover, really talented individuals are likely to attract the attention of the Church or nobility and to be drawn away and trained for the fine art field. The primitive artist has no such feeling of inferiority. The art in which he participates forms a continuum of skill and merit extending from the most precious and sacred objects to casually decorated tools. The artist and his work find their places in this continuum simply on the basis of excellence. Talented individuals are not drawn away from the primitive peasant community since the lure of cities is lacking. Even if an especially good sculptor is invited to come to a chief's village to execute a commission, ties of kin and property draw him back to his ancestral village as soon as the work is finished.

The societies to which primitive artists belong are usually much more rigidly organized than civilized groups, especially as regards the division of labor. There are always men's and women's crafts and regulations as to what materials may be used by each sex. Thus, with very rare exceptions, work in wood, stone, and metal is carried on exclusively by men, work in clay and fiber of all sorts by women. No woman can become a carver and no man a weaver, unless he chooses to relinquish his masculinity. In addition, the more advanced "uncivilized" groups recognize the economic advantages of craft monopolies and often conserve technical knowledge within kin groups. Thus among the Imerina in Madagascar the knowledge of how to make *ikat* cloth was limited to women of the noble clan, while in Africa such skills as brass casting, iron working, or pottery making are often rigidly guarded clan property.

These limitations are responsible for the not infrequent phenomenon of two or more totally different art styles coexisting in a single primitive society with little or no influence upon each other. Thus the tribes of British Columbia had a strong and elaborate animal art executed by men in wood, bone, and stone. Their totem poles are a familiar example. At the same time there was an only slightly less elaborate angular geometric art whose designs were interpreted as representations of plants and inanimate objects. This was executed by women in basketry. The two arts differed so completely that, if their provenance were not known, they would be ascribed to different North American design areas. Women's designs never appear on men's work while men's designs have influenced the women's artistic products at only one point, in the Chilkat blankets. In these the men painted the designs for the blankets on boards and the women then executed them in textile. The painted patterns made no allowance for the limitations usually imposed by textile media and their execution called for extreme technical skill on the part of the weaver. The whole procedure seems to have been a very late development and must be classed as a bit of virtuosity in no way characteristic of primitive aesthetics.

A somewhat similar situation existed in the North American Plains where an animal art in painting, executed by men, flourished side by side with an elaborate angular geometric art executed by women in quills, beads, and paint. Many other examples of such plurality of style could be cited, including even a few cases in which different styles characterize the work of different clans or other groups within a tribe. However, it is a curious fact that wherever a free naturalistic style and an angular geometric one coexist in the same society, the free style will be executed by men, the more constricted geometric style by women. An obvious reason for this can be seen in the preoccupation of women with textile manufacture, with its technical limitations, but it is not impossible that there are deeper psychological causes.

Primitive societies make no distinction between the artist and the artisan. With a very few exceptions such as the Chilkat blankets previously mentioned, the same individual both designs and executes and takes an equal pride in both skills. Because of the rigid social delimitation of his activities, he normally works in only one or two media and with a limited range of art forms. However, his technical control within this limited field is often of a high order. The effectiveness of primitive tools is considerably underrated by those who have never seen them in use. Surprisingly good work can be done with stone, bone, and tooth implements, and the main difference between these and metal tools lies in the increased time, effort, and manual skill required of the craftsman. Since the primitive artist is rarely interested in mass production and has no conception of the value of time per se, these limitations do not trouble him. Thus the Marquesans had learned how to cut basalt with rats' teeth and carved small, highly conventionalized images out of this highly refractory material. I was told that the making of such an image would take all of a man's spare time for from six months to a year.

Where as in Africa, iron is already in use, the primitive artist's equipment is usually little if at all inferior to that of the European artist in Gothic or even Classical times. The local tools may seem ineffective to a European but this is often due to his lack of muscular habits associated with their use. Thus in Madagascar I was much puzzled by the long handles and seemingly clumsy curved blades of the knives used in carving spoons and other small objects. When I discovered that the handle of the knife was held in the carver's armpit and the object pressed and turned against the blade, the utility of these features became obvious.

It has already been said that in most primitive societies no distinction is made between arts and crafts, and the artist's training is essentially that of a craftsman. The boy picks up a knowledge of how to handle his tools and of the artistic conventions of his group by observing work in progress. If he shows real promise, some established expert, often an older relative, will take him under his wing and put the finishing touches to his technical education. When the expert enjoys teaching or when, less frequently, there is an actual system of apprenticeship in which the master is paid for imparting his knowledge, regular ateliers may develop. In most of the more elaborate and professionalized primitive arts it is possible to recognize various pieces as the work of such and such a master or one of his pupils much as one can recognize a Renaissance painting as belonging to the school of so and so.

186

In spite of the tendency towards professionalism which characterizes all of the more elaborate primitive arts, the artist in such societies is assured of a considerably more intelligent and participant audience than he finds in our own. If one man in a primitive community carves or paints, all other men in his social group will usually do the same. The genius rises from a plateau of fellow craftsmen who may be less gifted but who have an intimate knowledge of his aims and of the techniques available for their fulfillment. Under these conditions virtuosity acquires a new value. The skill displayed with brush or chisel becomes in itself a source of aesthetic satisfaction to those accustomed to handle the brush or chisel. Problems of design and color arrangement are similarly familiar and the skill shown in solving them becomes in itself a source of intellectual pleasure. The primitive artist really works for an audience of other artists, thus simplifying his problems of communication. All this is in sharp contrast with the European practitioner of fine art, whose problems and techniques are almost completely unknown to his audience. The only conscious basis upon which this audience can judge his work is that of the accuracy with which he has reproduced the appearance of things. The extreme stress on naturalism which has characterized European fine art during the last three hundred years must be interpreted at least in part as an attempt to improve communication between the increasingly professional artist and the increasingly technically ignorant layman.

Primitive art is always conventional and stylized. That this is not due to any lack of technical skill on the part of the artist is demonstrated by the ease with which such artists turn out reasonably good naturalistic work as soon as the presence of Europeans provides a market for it. The real problem here is why a particular set of conventions was developed in the first place. While unique factors such as the presence at a particular time and place of a genius whose work influenced subsequent developments must be recognized as a partial explanation of particular conventions, there are more general causes. These fall into two groups, technological and psychological.

Although primitive artists have the skill required for naturalistic representations, it requires much time and labor to reproduce the exact appearance of any object. Moreover, this appearance usually leaves something to be desired from the point of view of artistic composition. The comments on this of one of my Marquesan friends, Huapuani, deserve to be repeated. His reaction to pictures of eighteenth-century European statuary was that it was technically clever but aesthetically barren. He felt that the superior tools of Europeans had made it possible for their artists to avoid the real problems of creative art by retreating into an exact and unimaginative reproduction of externals. What, he asked reasonably, was the point of making something that looked exactly like a woman if it did not feel like one or smell like one. The primitive artist learns to convey the idea of woman by a simplified image which is not only easier to execute but which also lends itself better to manipulation in terms of design. The convention becomes both a labor-saving device and a way to heightened aesthetic satisfaction.

The development of conventions is further aided by the fact that most of the presentations employed in primitive art are generic rather than individual. They are intended to convey the general idea woman, tree, or bear rather than that of a particular woman, tree, or bear. Portraiture in primitive art is excessively rare and when it does occur is usually limited to portraits of the dead. Here it strengthens the bond between the image and the original and makes the ghost more readily accessible to prayers and offerings. A similarly close bond between the image and a living original is fraught with great danger to the subject since injury done to the image is likely to be transferred to him. Our own traditional magic of the waxen man would be a case in point.

Even if there were no fear of magic, primitive technology makes the use of models exceedingly difficult. Primitive artists normally design and execute in the same final medium, the only significant exception being in metal casting by the cire-perdue process. Constant reference to a living subject thus becomes almost impossible. Even the most obliging model could hardly be expected to hold a pose while his portrait was carved from a log with a stone chisel. The primitive artist has to work from memory, and this in turn leads to a skill in visualization foreign to most Europeans.

All the primitive artists of my acquaintance have regarded the

European system of letting the design grow under the hand as nothing short of ridiculous. Before beginning work they clearly picture to themselves not only how the object will look from every possible direction but also how it will look in the particular place or under the particular circumstances in which it will be used. A few experiments in changing the lighting and elevation of almost any primitive mask or figure will make this clear. The mask which seems dull and inanimate when lying horizontal on a table becomes vibrant with force when seen as it is meant to be seen, standing vertically at the height of a tall man's head with lighting from above. Moreover, in making his design, the artist keeps constantly in mind the qualities of the material in which his work is to be executed. If it is to be in wood, he thinks in wood, with no intervention of pencil and paper.

To achieve such clear preliminary visualization of the finished work takes long practice but it is worth the effort. Once the composition is clear in the artist's mind he can proceed to execute almost as a mechanical matter. Like Michelangelo, his task becomes simply "freeing the statue from the marble." The ability to visualize often becomes in itself a matter of pride and a basis for exhibitionistic behavior. If the Marquesan artist was carving a bowl he would shape the object completely and give it the highest possible polish before beginning to carve so that any change of his design as well as any slip of his chisel would be evident in the finished work. Both the Marquesans and the related Maori of New Zealand developed their abilities to conceive and memorize designs without the aid of sketches to a point rarely if ever equalled by Europeans. In New Zealand in particular it was not uncommon for the artist to conceive his design in terms of a field larger than the object on which the design was to be carved, then reproduce on the object only those parts of the total design which fell within the outline of the object when this was superimposed on the original imaginary field. As a further bit of virtuosity two or three designs conceived in terms of fields of different sizes or shapes might be superimposed upon each other in the decoration of a single object. To the European the results are often bewildering.

This method of composition opens the way for a subtle type of conventionalization which is foreign to our own artistic concepts but which finds parallels in the arts of Asiatic civilizations. When one attempts to make an accurate copy of any work of primitive art one discovers that, in addition to the obvious conventions of form and design, there is a subtle and illusive convention in the quality of the lines and irregular curves employed by the artist. As far as I can discover, the Japanese are the only people who have been sensitive enough to recognize this fact and to develop an extensive classification of these features as they appear in their own art. Such conventions presumably result from the development of certain muscular habits during the artist's apprenticeship as a copyist of other men's work and are comparable to those embodied in various styles of writing: Gothic, Arabic, or Chinese. They are also comparable to the individual tricks of chisel or brush work which aid in identifying the products of our own matsers, but in primitive art they tend to be characteristic of an art style itself rather than of an individual. Their influence is so strong that even when the native artist attempts to copy European designs they survive and make his affiliations recognizable. The development of this sort of convention is quite impossible as long as the artist aims at exact reproduction of what he sees, since no two curves in nature are ever exactly the same. Its presence in nearly all primitive arts is an additional proof of the degree to which these arts are consciously divorced from naturalism.

So much for the technological factors leading to conventionalization in primitive art. Turning to the psychological factors, I believe they may be summed up in the simple statement that the primitive artist tries to represent his subject as he and his society think of it, not as they see it. Working from memory as he does, he draws from two sources, his memory of the thing to be represented and his memory of how the work of other artists who have tried to represent the same thing looked. His memory images are only partly visual. They are distorted by all sorts of evaluations based on the relation of the thing represented to the artist's society and culture. Thus the artist's mental image of a bear inevitably exaggerates such details as the teeth and claws, highly pertinent features of the animal if one is hunting him. This image also may include details of the animal's anatomy which are invisible when the animal is alive. Thus many North American Indian pictures of game animals show not only the external features, often caught with considerable skill, but also the heart and aorta. These are included because they are, in native tradition, the seat of the animal's life and also, in practical terms, the hunter's target.

Primitive art is thus abstract art, in the sense that the artist selects or abstracts those features of his subject which seem to him most worthy of emphasis. His work is thus comparable in some respects to that of our own abstractionists, but there is one important difference. The modern abstract artist tends to base his selection upon his personal reaction to his subject and, as a result, his compositions are sometimes unintelligible to the greater part of his audience. The primitive artist's abstraction rests upon the consensus of opinion of his society, and his work is correspondingly intelligible to his audience.

To Europeans, the most striking feature of primitive arts as a group is probably the freedom which they show in the treatment of the human body. Until very recent times our own artists have hesitated to use the human figure as a basis for abstract design, partly as a result of the Classical tradition, partly as a result of religious attitudes. The primitive artist feels free to exaggerate, distort, or suppress any anatomical features and to treat the body simply as a starting point in the development of conceptually significant compositions. Thus New Guinea masks and figures from the Sepik River area show fantastic exaggeration of the nose, understandable when one learns that big noses are regarded here as indications of virility. In the Marquesas Islands the heads and faces of images were worked out in elaborate detail while the rest of the body was reduced to a few essential planes and masses. This was because the head was regarded as the seat of the individual's *mana* or spiritual power while the eyes, ears, nose, and mouth symbolized the senses. The conventionalized representations of these organs conveyed the idea of man alert in the universe to a native audience, and at the same time permitted of more decorative treatment than an accurate representation of the same organs would have done.

In conclusion, it should be repeated that primitive art is not naive, nor technically deficient. Its curious associations of ideas are always logical and understandable in terms of the artist's culture. Neither are its tendencies towards abstraction and conventionalization due to failure to perceive natural forms or inability to reproduce them with fair accuracy. The primitive arts represent different lines of evolution in the universal search for beauty. It is even questionable whether their conventionalization detracts seriously from the artist's opportunity for self-expression. The conventions limit him in certain directions but they also serve to focus his creative abilities on problems of pure form, organization, and design. He may be permitted to use only a limited number of motifs but, freed from the demands of naturalism, he can treat these with intellectual clarity. The symbolism of the forms which he employs is so familiar to him and to his audience that he can convey innumerable ideas and their emotional effects without detracting from the formal aesthetic value of his work. Since the European observer is ignorant of the symbolic meanings of primitive art, its appreciation is for him an intellectual exercise which helps to clarify his understanding of aesthetics.

The Writings of Ralph Linton

1917 With B. W. Hawkes. "A Pre-Lenape Site in New Jersey." Anthropological Publications of the Museum of the University of Pennsylvania 4, No. 3.

1917 Reply to "Review of 'A pre-Lenape site in New Jersey'." American Anthropologist 19, No. 1:144–47.

1922 The thunder ceremony of the Pawnee. Field Museum Leaflet 5, 19 pp. 4 pls.

1922 The sacrifice to the morning star by the Skidi Pawnee. Field Museum Leaflet 6, 18 pp. 1 pl.

1923 Purification of the sacred bundles, a ceremony of the Pawnee. Field Museum Leaflet 7, 11 pp., 1 pl.

1923 Annual ceremony of the Pawnee medicine men. Field Museum Leaflet 8, 20 pp., 2 pls.

1923 The material culture of the Marquesas Islands. B. P. Bishop Museum, Memoirs, Vol. 8, No. 5, pp. 263–471, pls. XL–LXXIV. Honolulu.

1924 "Origin of the Plains earth lodge." American Anthropologist 26, No. 2:247–57.

1924 "Totemism and the A. E. F." American Anthropologist 26, No. 2:296–300.

1924 "Significance of certain traits in North American maize culture." American Anthropologist 26, No. 3:345–49.

1924 Use of tobacco among North American Indians. Field Museum Leaflet 15, 27 pp., 6 pls.

1925 Archaeology of the Marquesas Islands. B. P. Bishop Museum Bulletin 23. 187 pp., 30 figs., 15 pls. Honolulu.

1925 "Marquesan culture." American Anthropologist 27, No. 3:474–78.

1926 "Degeneration of human figures used in Polynesian decorative art." Journal of the Polynesian Society 33, No. 4:321–324.

1926 Ethnology of Polynesia and Micronesia. Field Museum of Natural History, Dept. of Anthropology Guide, PL 6. Chicago.

1926 "Origin of the Skidi Pawnee sacrifice to the morning star." American Anthropologist 28, No. 3:457–66.

1927 "Witches of Andilamena." Atlantic Monthly 139:191–96 (February).

1927 "Overland." Atlantic Monthly 140:808–17 (December).

1927 "Report on work of Field Museum expedition in Madagascar." American Anthropologist 29, No. 3:292–307.

1927 "Rice, a Malagasy tradition." American Anthropologist 29, No. 4:654–60.

1928 "Culture areas in Madagascar." American Anthropologist 30:363–90.

1928   "White magic." Atlantic Monthly 141:721–35 (June).

1928   "Desert." Atlantic Monthly 142:588–600 (November).

1928   "Market day in Madagascar." Asia 28, No. 5:386–89.

1930   "Use of tobacco in Madagascar" *in* Tobacco and its Use in Africa by B. Laufer, W. D. Hambly, and Ralph Linton. Field Museum Leaflet 29, pp. 38–43. Chicago.

1933   "Primitive art." The American Magazine of Art 26, No. 1:17–24, 4 pls. Washington, American Federation of Arts.

1933   The Tanala, a hill tribe of Madagascar. Field Museum of Natural History, Anthropological Series 22. 334 pp., 35 figs. Chicago.

1935   "The Comanche sun dance." American Anthropologist 37, No. 3:420–28.

1936   With R. Redfield, and M. J. Herskovits. "Memorandum for the study of acculturation." American Anthropologist 38, No. 1:149–52.

1936   "Error in anthropology" *in* The Story of Human Error, pp. 292–321. New York, Appleton-Century.

1936   The study of man, an introduction. New York, Appleton-Century.

1937   "On theory and practice." University of Toronto Quarterly 7:113–25.

1937   "One hundred per cent American." American Mercury 40:427–29 (April).

1938   "Culture, society and the individual." Journal of Abnormal and Social Psychology 33, No. 4:425–36.

1938   "The present status of Anthropology." Science 87:241–48.

1938   "One hundred per cent American." Readers Digest 32, No. 191:31–33.

1939   "Culture sequences in Madagascar." Transactions of the New York Academy of Sciences 1, No. 7:116–17.

1939   "The effects of culture on mental and emotional processes." Research Publications of the Assoc. for Research in Nervous and Mental Disease, pp. 293–304.

1939   Foreword, pp. v–xviii; "Marquesan culture," pp. 197–250; "The Tanala of Madagascar," pp. 251–90; *in* The Individual and His Society, by Abram Kardiner. New York, Columbia University Press.

1940   (Ed.) Acculturation in seven American Indian Tribes. New York, Appleton-Century.

1940   "Crops, soils, and culture in America" *in* The Maya and their Neighbors, pp. 32–40. New York, Appleton-Century.

1940   "Psychology and Anthropology." Journal of Social Philosophy 5, No. 2:115–26.

1940   "A neglected aspect of social organization." American Journal of Sociology 45, No. 6:870–86.

1940   "The prospects of Western civilization" *in* War in the Twentieth Century (W. W. Waller, ed.), pp. 533–56. New York, Dryden Press.

1941   "Primitive art." Kenyon Review 3, No. 1:34–51, 4 pls. Gambier, Ohio.

1941 "Some functional, social and biological aspects of offenses and offenders." Federal Probation 5, No. 2:17–21.

1941 "Some recent developments in Southwestern archaeology." Transactions of the New York Academy of Sciences 4, No. 2:66–69.

1942 "Age and sex categories." American Sociological Review 7, No. 5:589–603.

1942 "Land tenure in aboriginal America," in The Changing Indian, pp. 42–54. Norman, University of Oklahoma Press.

1942 Estudio del Hombre (trans. by Daniel F. Rubín de la Borbolla). Mexico City, Fondo de Cultura Economica.

1943 "Culture sequences in Madagascar." Studies in the Anthropology of Oceania and Asia, in memory of Roland Barrage Dixon, pp. 72–80. Cambridge, Peabody Museum.

1943 "Nativistic movements." American Anthropologist 45, No. 2:230–40.

1943 O Homem: Uma Introdução à Antropologia (trans. by Lavinia Vilela). São Paulo, Livraria Martins Editôra.

1944 "North American cooking pots." American Antiquity 9, No. 4:369–80.

1944 "Nomad raids and fortified pueblos." American Antiquity 10, No. 1:28–32.

1944 With Adelin Linton. "Say, how'd you like the girls?" McCall's Magazine, pp. 14 (August).

1945 The cultural background of personality. New York, Appleton-Century.

1945 Foreword to a Chinese Village by Martin C. Yang, pp. v–vii. New York, Columbia University Press.

1945 Cultura y Personalidad (trans. by Javier Romero). México, D. F., Fondo de Cultura Economica.

1945 Foreword, pp. v–xiii; "The Comanche," pp. 47–80; in The Psychological Frontiers of Society, by Abram Kardiner. Columbia University Press.

1945 (Ed.) The Science of man in the world crisis. New York, Columbia University Press.

1945 "The scope and aims of anthropology," pp. 3–18; "Present world conditions in cultural perspective," pp. 201–21; in The Science of Man in the World Crisis. New York, Columbia University Press.

1946 Introduction to Journey to Accompong by Katherine Dunham. New York, Henry Holt.

1946 With Paul Wingert and Rene d'Harnoncourt. Arts of the South Seas. New York, Museum of Modern Art.

1946 "Why you like what you like." House Beautiful, p. 154 (December).

1947 "The vanishing American Negro." American Mercury, pp. 133–139 (January). Reprinted in Negro Digest, pp. 33–39 (August).

1947 With Adelin Linton. Man's way from cave to skyscraper. New York, Harper & Bros.

1947 With Abram Kardiner. "The change from dry to wet rice culture in Tanala-Betsileo" in Readings in Social Psychology, pp. 46–55. New York, Henry Holt.

1947 "Concepts of role and status" *in* Readings in Social Psychology, pp. 330–67.

1949 (Ed.) Most of the world: the peoples of Africa, Latin America and the East today. New York, Columbia University Press.

1949 "Problems of status personality" *in* Culture and Personality (S. S. Sargent and M. W. Smith, eds.). New York, Viking Fund Publication.

1949 "The natural history of the family" *in* The Family, Its Function and Destiny (Ruth Nanda Anshen, ed.), pp. 18–38. New York, Harper and Bros.

1949 "The personality of peoples." Scientific American, pp. 11–15. (August).

1949 With Adelin Linton. We gather together, the story of Thanksgiving. New York, Henry Schuman.

1950 "An anthropologist views Point IV." American Perspective, pp. 113–21 (Spring). Washington, D.C., Foundation for Foreign Affairs.

1950 "An anthropologist views the Kinsey report." Scientific Monthly, pp. 282–85 (May).

1950 With Adelin Linton. Halloween. New York, Henry Schuman.

1951 With Adelin Linton. The lore of birthdays. New York, Henry Schuman.

1951 "New light on ancient America." Scientific Monthly 72, No. 5 (May).

1951 "Halloween." Scientific American 185, No. 4 (October).

1951 "The concept of national character" *in* Personality and Political Crisis (A. H. Stanton and S. E. Perry, eds.). Glencoe, Illinois, Free Press.

1952 "Women in the family" *in* Women, Society, and Sex (Johnson E. Fairchild, ed.). New York, Sheridan House.

1952 "Universal ethical principles: an anthropological view" *in* Moral Principles of Action (Ruth Nanda Anshen, ed.). Science of Culture Series, Vol. VI. New York, Harper and Bros.

1952 "Culture and personality factors affecting economic growth" *in* The Progress of Underdeveloped Areas (Bert Hoselitz, ed.), pp. 73 ff. Chicago, Ill., University of Chicago Press.

1953 "An anthropological view of economics" *in* Goals of Economic Life (A. Dudley Ward, ed.), pp. 305 ff. New York, Harper and Bros.

1953 "The proper study." Saturday Review of Literature, pp. 38–39 (April 4th).

1955 The Tree of Culture. New York, Alfred A. Knopf. (An abridged version in paperback is available.)

1956 Culture and Mental Disorders. Springfield, Illinois, Charles C. Thomas, Publisher, edited by George Devereux.

1958 "Primitive Art" *in* The Sculpture of Africa by Eliot Elisofon, New York, Frederick A. Praeger.